The Abney Method to Owning a Dog

by

Don Abney

authorHOUSE®

AuthorHouse™
1663 Liberty Drive, Suite 200
Bloomington, IN 47403
www.authorhouse.com
Phone: 1-800-839-8640

First published by AuthorHouse   8/4/2008

ISBN: 978-1-4343-9029-5 (e)
ISBN: 978-1-4343-9031-8 (sc)
ISBN: 978-1-4343-9030-1 (hc)

Library of Congress Control Number: 2008904648

Printed in the United States of America
Bloomington, Indiana

This book is printed on acid-free paper.

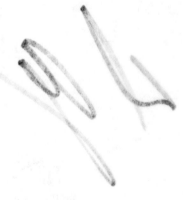

Dedicated to the memory of

Donald J. Abney, Sr.

The man who taught me canine training and

the values that I live by today.

Thanks, Dad.

Acknowledgments

Your effort and dedication made it possible for me to accomplish the contents of this book.

Kathleen Abney, wife, partner, photographer and pre-editor, with patience and understanding of my shortcomings

James (Pete) Hendry, DVM, General Animal Hospital, Covington, Louisiana

Greg Labranche, DVM, General Animal Hospital, Covington, Louisiana

Susan Strain, DVM, Claiborne Hill Veterinary Clinic, Covington, Louisiana

Representative Mike Strain, DVM, Claiborne Hill Veterinary Clinic, Covington, Louisiana

Tommi Pugh, DVM, Claiborne Hill Veterinary Clinic, Covington, Louisiana

George Strain, PhD, Louisiana State University, Baton Rouge, Louisiana

Lawrence Myers, DVM, MS, PhD, Auburn University, Auburn, Alabama

AND

To all of the dedicated professionals before me, whose trials and efforts have provided me with the tools to make my methods a success.

THANK YOU!

Table of Contents

About Don Abney

Born in Louisiana, Don recalls that his first dog was a wild dog that was caught in the swamps of Louisiana by his father on a hunting trip. The dog was named Skippy because of a slight limp he had when he was captured. After watching the dog being handled by his father, Don was taught how to handle the dog and teach it to do certain tricks. This was the very beginning of his dog-training career. As he grew older, the dog training was left behind for other interests and pursuits, but it was never abandoned.

After serving in the military, he went on to pursue a career in electronics with the telephone company, and then a career in law enforcement. During these years, he would help others with the problems they were encountering with their dogs, and present instructions on how to correct whatever problem they had encountered.

The decision was made to offer his services to the public and thus began ABCANTRA (Abney's Canine Training) which continues in operation today. An Internet Web site, *http://www.abcantra.com*, was designed to offer free information and help for dog owners.

Listed below are some of the accomplishments Don has attained:

- **Master Trainer certification** in obedience, tracking (human and game), search and rescue, detector dogs, and behavior modification since 1980.

- Court-certified **expert** in the field of canine training and tracking, through the Criminal District Courts of New Orleans, Louisiana. — December 10, 1998, by Judge Julian Parker.

- United Kennel Club (UKC) Junior Showmanship Judge.

- United Kennel Club (UKC) all-breed Conformation Judge.

- American Kennel Club (AKC) *Canine Good Citizen* evaluator.

- Licensed by the Drug Enforcement Agency, as a researcher in the field of canine training.

- Studies in dog psychology, animal behavior, breeding and genetics, canine nutrition, and health care.

- Experienced in handling dangerous, vicious, and nuisance animals.

- Founding member and trainer of Louisiana Search and Rescue Dogs, Inc. 1989–1996.

- Retired reserve lieutenant, St. Tammany Parish Sheriff's Office— Search and Rescue Division.

- Author of **The Louisiana Catahoula Leopard Dog,** a book on the history, breeding, and care of the Louisiana Catahoula Leopard Dog.

- Owner, handler, and trainer of "Ladyhawke," the *first* registered Louisiana Catahoula Leopard Dog to be certified in search and rescue, and narcotics detection to be commissioned by law enforcement.

- Recipient of the *"Service Champion Award"* for outstanding work in community service, presented by the National Association of Louisiana Catahoulas.

- Awarded *"Excellence in Training"* by Sigma Chemical Corporation.

- Author of the **Canine Tracking Guide,** a book on how to train a dog to follow a track.

- Certified breeder of registered Louisiana Catahoula Leopard Dogs since 1985. *(N.A.L.C.)*

- *President* of the **American Catahoula Association** – 1998–2004.

- **President** of the ***Catahoula Owner, Breeder, and Research Association*** **(COBRA),** a United Kennel Club single-breed organization.

- **President** of the ***Great Southern Kennel Club,*** a multi-breed ***United Kennel Club*** organization).

Introduction

The majority of information contained in training books is very similar in its method. The trainers who write the books are giving you the knowledge of their experiences. In doing so, they forget that the majority of folks owning dogs do not intend to exhibit them. The owner only wants to have a dog that will come when called and have some manners that would make it acceptable to their friends, family, and the general public.

Inside you will find that I have tried to create a guide for the general dog owner. It is not intended to create a show dog or an award-winning dog, but to give you the groundwork, if that is your desire. This book is intended to help in choosing your dog, understanding your dog, training your dog in basic obedience, and accomplishing some of the general skills that are needed to be a successful dog owner. Dogs are living, loving creatures that make every effort to understand humans and try to please us by fitting into our pack. If you want the bond often seen with some other dog owners, you have to make an effort to understand the dog.

Choosing the right breed of dog for your lifestyle is more important than choosing the type of car you are going to drive. Most people will spend weeks studying vehicles before making a decision as to which one will suit their lifestyle, taste, and pocketbook. Choosing a dog should be done in the same manner. Unfortunately, some dogs are chosen as a spontaneous thought, a spur-of-the-moment decision, without any real thought going into it.

I am a breeder of Louisiana Catahoula Leopard Dogs, and I have never seen an ugly puppy in any of my litters. Puppies are cute, and this is what causes most people to take a dog from someone wanting to get rid of an unwanted pup or litter. It is also the way those looking for a dog are swayed to purchase a dog that is not really what they desire. For example, have you ever seen a pet shop that displays grown dogs? All of the display cages are placed in a position so the public may see the cute puppies that are available. People giving away puppies will show up in parking lots with a boxful of cute, unwanted puppies. Shoppers passing these puppies will stop and look at the puppies and admire how cute they are. Then the thoughts of what may happen to those puppies cause them to take one home, even though they were not looking for a puppy.

I am not saying that people who take free puppies are irresponsible dog owners, but most do not think beyond the puppy stage before they take the puppy. Those who are giving them away are not bad people either. You must consider, though, if these puppies are being given away, this was not a planned litter, and the adult dogs should have been spayed or neutered. It is this type of irresponsible breeding that is overpopulating the world with unwanted dogs. If you do not want puppies, do not allow the chance for a breeding.

Owning a dog takes time away from other things that you could be doing. There will be times that are inconvenient for you when you may have to go to the veterinarian's office. You may have to change some plans because of your dog. You may have to spend a little extra money to board your dog while you are away on vacation, or contact someone to take care of your dog while you are away.

Owning a dog is a responsibility that must be considered and accepted before bringing one into your life. Many dog lovers do not own dogs. Why? Their lifestyles do not permit them to own a dog. They have accepted the fact that a dog would be a responsibility that could interfere with their lives, and they have eliminated the possibility of dog ownership.

Not everyone needs to own a dog, and in some cases, there are those who should not own a dog. If you have decided that you want to own a dog, this book will help you in making some of the decisions that you may have overlooked in your quest for dog ownership.

Chapter 1
Choosing Your Puppy

You have had a meeting with the family, and the decision has been made to purchase a puppy. Everyone in the family is going to accept some of the responsibility of raising and training this puppy. Right?

Or perhaps you are single, live alone, and you want a dog for company. Do you know what you are getting into?

Owning a dog is an added responsibility. It is like bringing a child into the home, but it does not talk, cannot help with the housework, will not clean the yard, will not tidy up the garage or wash the car. However, it will need all the other things a child needs. It will need attention, guidance, care, understanding, training, affection, and discipline. If the family is willing to comply with all of these needs and share in the responsibilities of caring for the dog, you are ready to choose a puppy. Do not forget, I said *everyone* in the family. If everyone does not use the same commands and method of training and corrections, you will end up with a confused dog. After it becomes confused by all the mixed signals, you will be seeking a professional trainer or a new place for your dog to live.

Since the decision has been made to acquire a puppy, it would be crucial to decide which type of dog you are going to choose. Consider some of the following things that may help you in deciding what type of dog would fit into your family.

Pure or Mixed

"Should I spend the money to get a purebred dog, go to the local shelter and rescue an abandoned dog, or just take a mixed-breed puppy from someone selling or giving them away?" I have been asked this question as many times as I have been asked my name. The ultimate decision lies with you and your pocketbook. Let us take it in the order generally asked.

Purebred dogs. What you have with most purebred dogs is a generation of breeding dogs that have been chosen to produce certain elements of ability and behavior, such as working, hunting, guarding, color, size, structure, and temperament. Numerous hours of study have gone into creating the dogs with these traits, dogs that remain appealing to the eye. What you are paying for with a purebred dog is the time that goes into creating them, caring for them, and nurturing them until they are ready to leave the litter. Breeding in this manner aids in producing a dog that fits its overall breed description. In addition to ability, you also have health, stamina, temperament, and someone who knows the breed and your specific puppy if there are any problems. You will have some idea of what to expect from the dog.

Shelter/rescued dogs. I do not want to offend any of the people who are attempting to rescue animals. I think they have taken a great step in the adoption program, but—as most of these people will tell you—you seldom know what type of dog you are getting. You often do not know if the dog was abandoned or mistreated. You may not know what has been done to or for the dog prior to being rescued. How many times does a dog get returned to a shelter before someone finally keeps it or takes it somewhere else and lets it go, only to be someone else's problem? If you adopt a shelter dog, place that dog into an obedience (manners) training class. Do not wait until the dog has you—literally or figuratively—backed into a corner and you need help. Adopt the dog; enter a class.

Mixed breeds. There are a great number of mixed-breed dogs that do very well in today's society and environment. The only thing missing for the average owner of a mixed-breed dog is knowledge about what is inside the dog. Determining which traits are dominant over the others can be difficult. In other words, it is a guess. If you were to acquire a mixed-breed dog that was known to have been a cross of German Shepherd and Poodle, you might not know what the temperament or attitude of this dog is going to be. Just because it looks like a shepherd does not mean it will automatically act like one. There is a guessing game in these types of breeding. You do not know which genes got crossed. Of course, all purebred dogs were mixed breeds at some time in their beginning, but it was the continuous selection of genetic differences that was achieved to recreate the same patterns. With a mixed-breed litter, you can't tell which is which. Some may look like poodles, others like shepherds, and still others unknown. It is just a guess.

To some, this explanation may sound lopsided, but I am a breeder who takes the time to place all of my puppies before any breeding takes place. I have owned mixed-breed dogs, and I have had great success with them. I have trained a great number of mixed-breed dogs that are doing well. It was the early training that nipped any problems in the bud. As a matter of point, my first dog as a child was a wild puppy that my father caught in the woods. A veterinarian said it may have been a cross between a collie and a spitz, but who knows? It was a great dog! My dad took the time with the dog, as soon as it came into the house, to teach it proper manners. This is where I first learned the art of dog training.

What breed of dog do you want? All dogs look good on television and in the movies, because they have been groomed to make the best presentation possible. Visual effects, aesthetics, are the most popular reason people buy a particular breed of dog. Then, when the dog is older and needs more care than they are willing to give, a problem ensues. They want to get rid of the dog.

You would not buy a car based solely on the way it looks, would you? You would want to know the make and model. What kind of reputation does it have? How much does it cost? What warranty comes with it? What is the length of the warranty? How much maintenance does it require? Are there any defects you should know about? Acquiring a dog is not much different. You should consider all of the various breeds that suit your eye and that of all your family members. Now research all of those breeds. Do not purchase a breed just because you like the way it looks. Impulse buying is one of the biggest pitfalls of dog ownership. Too often, a puppy is chosen because: (1) you think it is cute; (2) you are concerned for its welfare; or (3) you've wanted a dog, and this one is available at a price that is affordable.

Know what you are getting into. Investigate the size the dog will be when it is fully grown. Puppies are cute, but they do grow up. You should be prepared for this. You should also be prepared for a place to keep your full-grown dog. Puppies do not need a lot of room, but a grown dog does. It must have adequate room to exercise, and it must have a shelter where it can retreat from the rain and the cold. Here are just a few of the things you should consider:

- How large will it be when fully grown?
- What type of coat/hair will it have?
- What is its activity level?
- What are its social tolerances?
- What are its disease tolerances?
- Are there any genetic abnormalities? If so, what are they?
- Where will it live?
- How much care will it require?
- Where will it stay when you want to get away or go on vacation?

Size is something that most people pay little attention to when it concerns a dog. If you look at a large dog that has a good breadth, you should be advised that it probably takes a considerable amount of food to keep it looking that way. Food is important to everyone, including your dog. You should consider the quantity of food that will be required to keep your dog healthy. Along with quantity is quality. Your leftovers are not a healthy diet for your dog, because there would be required nutrients missing from its diet. If you need a garbage disposal, buy one. Quality dog food may cost a little more than the bargain brands, but you will not use as much. If you cannot afford to keep your dog in top condition, you should reconsider owning a dog.

Food alone is not your only maintenance concern. There are visits to the veterinarian for shots, checkups, and those incidents where nothing should go wrong, but does. There are trips to the pet store for toys to keep it from chewing up all the furniture or the outside of your house. There are collars and leads, and the list goes on. I want you to be aware of some of the responsibilities of owning a dog. You should be certain this is what you want. If you think your dog will never have any problems that would warrant an unscheduled visit to the veterinarian's office, think again. It happens to someone every day. It is not cheap or easy to keep up with a dog.

What coat length will this dog have when it is grown? The longer the hair on a dog, the more brushing it requires. If you are lax about brushing, the hair will become knotted. You will be at a grooming salon or a veterinarian's office to have your dog clipped, because you cannot get the knots out. Grooming or brushing should be a regular occurrence. Shorthaired dogs require some brushing, but longhaired dogs require a schedule of regular brushing. If you consider maintenance or expense to be a problem, then you should not own a dog.

What about cost? You should consider how much you are willing to pay for a dog. This is the only "one-time" thing that will occur with your dog. Along with the cost of the dog, you should inquire about guarantees. Any breeder worth his salt will give you a guarantee. He should be willing to replace the puppy or take the puppy back if there is a serious problem. Most people do not ask about guarantees when purchasing a puppy. Either they are afraid of offending the breeder or they just do not know to ask. Don't be afraid to ask! For example, if you purchased a candy bar and found it to be spoiled, you wouldn't eat it, would you? No. You would ask for another bar or your money back. Do the same when purchasing a dog. Get that guarantee. You may not need it, but, if you do, you will have it.

What is the activity level of this breed? How much exercise will it require? Just because you let your dog out of the house to relieve itself does not mean that this is all of the exercise it needs. You must be willing to take it for a walk or a run. If it is an active type of dog, you will be sorry you do not take it for those walks. Remember the reference to eating furniture and houses? Generally, this is the reason for that type of behavior. Dogs need exercise, and you must be willing to help them get what they need. This includes those rainy nights when you feel like no man alive should be outside.

"Social tolerances" refers to how well this breed behaves around people and other animals. This is particularly important if you intend to walk your dog or take it along on trips. Training will help with some of the issues but socialization is more important than most owners believe. You must make an effort to socialize your dog. Ask a breeder or veterinarian if there is any genetic relationship to socialization. There are inherited traits in some breeding lines that will make some dogs harder to socialize than others. If the breeder is breeding for an aggressive type of dog, socializing will be more difficult. Even if you are purchasing a dog for security around your home, the dog *must* be socialized. It should be tolerant of people and other animals. It is up to you to socialize this animal. The lack of socialization is one of the primary causes of dogfights and dog bites. The dog does not understand the human behavior and goes directly into its defense mode. The next thing you know, you are on the six o'clock news, because your dog has bitten a child. If you think maintenance is costly, wait until you see the bottom line in that lawsuit.

What diseases are common among your chosen breed? Some breeds are prone to diseases that are predisposed by genetic traits. Genetic inheritance is important, and it should be researched. Many dogs have some unwanted genetic trait. Some traits will seriously affect your dog, while others are not as serious.

Which sex do you want, male or female? The question as to which sex is better is a debate that has gone on for decades. I have seen great males and females of all breeds. A lot depends on the personality of each given dog. There are some things that you should consider when making your choice.

Males tend to go through a roller coaster ride of hormone imbalances. One day it is at the top of the hill, and the next day it's at the bottom. These rides can change the personality of the dog and lead to some confusion on the part of the owner. Marking his territory, and anything else he believes is his, can become a problem. It can be curtailed with training, but it can also be very nerve-wracking. Intact males tend to fight more than those that have been neutered. Neutering a dog that displays an aggressive temperament may change that temperament, provided the aggression is hormonally driven. If the aggression is caused by genetic predisposition, it will require intense training and continuous monitoring.

Females can be equally annoying when they come into heat every six months. Along with bleeding that comes with their cycle, they too can go through that roller coaster ride. When a female is in the peak of her heat cycle, there is only one thing that she wants, and that is to breed. A female in heat can attract males literally from a mile away. This could have unwanted visitors at your door, barking at your fence, and driving you crazy in general. This holds true for male and female visitors. There are females that are curious about other females in heat. If you spay your female, you will reduce these problems dramatically.

The above examples do not answer the question of which selection is better, but it gives you an idea of what to expect and what you may have to deal with. The ultimate decision lies with you and your preference. Keep in mind the purpose for which you are choosing this dog. If you intend to use it for work, remember that the intact female will be removed from its duties during the heat cycle to prevent an accidental breeding. That is a minimum of twenty-one days, twice each year, unless she is spayed.

When you have narrowed the decision to a few breeds, go to the library or search the Internet for in-depth information, such as inherited traits, temperament, size, and history of the breed. The library may not have information on some rare breeds of dogs, but it is a good place to start. Bookstores and pet shops may also be able to help you with your research. During your research, you may find that the breed you really want is not the one that you initially chose. Do not be surprised if you come home with a longer list than you started with.

Take some time to view a few dog shows or training classes. You will see many of the breeds that are available, and get a closer look at the breeds you may have chosen to become yours. Talk to the owners of the breeds you have chosen, and get their input on that breed. Find out who the breeder was, and contact him. Do not talk to just one breeder; talk to several. Keep in mind that you are researching and are not ready to buy. Let the breeders know this before you begin questioning them. You do not want to put the breeders in a selling or defensive posture, so let them know why you are calling. You want them to share their views of their particular breed. Ask each breeder why he is involved with this breed. His answer may help you in making the decision as to the breed of dog you really want.

I am directing you toward seeking a dog breeder, rather than choosing a dog from a pet shop. Most pet shops will not tell you where the puppy came from, and they cannot answer any questions about the litter or the pair of dogs that were bred. They cannot tell you any of the background on any of the puppies in their shop. Oh, they may be able to tell you some of the history of the breed, but you want to know as much as possible about that *particular* puppy. They will not know, because they were not the breeder.

If you have a problem with your puppy, you have little, if any, recourse with a pet shop. Pet shops do not always carry quality dogs.

I am not saying that a good dog cannot be purchased from a pet shop, but your chances of getting a good-quality dog are limited. You have only one choice, the one that is in front of you. In a litter of puppies, you have a greater number of choices.

I know of a case where a puppy was purchased from a pet store. This was an impulse purchase, so the pet store is not to blame for selling the puppy. That is a part of their business. The puppy appeared to be normal in every way until it was about a year old. The couple noticed that the dog began limping more and more. They brought it to their veterinarian, where it was diagnosed with hip problems. The couple contacted the pet shop, and they were told there was nothing the pet shop could do about the dog's problems. After all, it had been almost a year since the dog was purchased, and anything could have happened to cause this problem.

After many hours of research, the couple finally found out who the breeder was and made a phone call to him. Their problem was explained to this breeder. The couple indicated that they would like some assistance with getting the dog's hip problems repaired, since they wanted to keep the dog. The breeder hung up on them without a word. Apparently, this was a back yard breeder or a puppy mill. Here you have dogs with physical and psychological problems and owners without any recourse. This type of situation happens every day.

My primary interest lies with the dog. I want you to have the dog you want, but I want the dog to have a home where it will be happy, too. This is not always an easy thing to achieve. I feel that by telling you all of this in advance, you will be able to give some serious thought to owning a dog. There are too many dogs receiving bad publicity simply because owners did not take the time to understand the dogs and their needs. Too many breeds are singled out because of problems that are caused by humans. We, the people, decide that a breed is bad or vicious based on bad publicity. How often do you see any type of legislation protecting a dog? Generally, it is the public crying out for the banning of certain breeds.

Keep in mind that dog owners/lovers are in the minority of the general population. Because of that, we should strive to be better owners and breeders. It is not the dog's fault if an owner makes a dog respond in a manner that is not publicly acceptable. It is the owner's fault. I would hope that someday people would understand this, and they would have legislation passed against "bad dog owners" instead of the dogs. Dogs are not born mean. We make them that way.

Okay, I am off my soapbox now, and I will try to help you in making a selection.

You have arrived at the home of the breeder, and you are ready to view the litter. STOP! You will want to view the breeding pair first. Look at the sire (Dad) and the dam (Mom). This will be your guide as to what your dog should look like when it is grown. It will also be an indicator as to the type of care the dogs, and the puppies, are receiving. No one sees an ugly puppy. That is because all puppies are cute. Look at the adults first. Look at the living conditions of the dogs. Are they clean? Are the kennels and home clean? Are there any foul smells? Nursing bitches may have an odor about them because of the puppies' walking all over her. She and the puppies are the only exceptions. Do not make up excuses because you think the puppies are cute or because the price is a real bargain. What appears as a bargain now may not be a bargain later.

You have asked those important questions about guarantees, policy, problems you should be aware of, why those two dogs were bred, and the breeder has passed the test. Now it is time to pick a puppy. I cannot tell you which puppy to pick, but I can help you to decide. If you follow the instructions as closely as possible, they may help you decide which puppy to bring home. There are a few tests, like picking him up off the ground, that may require a little more strength and balance on your part, but the tests will work.

There are no guarantees that by using these tests you will get the perfect dog. I've been working with dogs for years, and I can assure you that the perfect dog only comes along once in a great while. These tests may assist you in making your decision, but there are other circumstances that could change the outcome of the tests after you make your selection. One is the amount of attention the dog receives. Dogs are pack animals, and they rely on their pack to give them comfort, safety, and assurance. Your place is pack leader, and it is up to you to set up the rules and guidelines for your new addition. Another circumstance is the amount of training, socialization, and exercise your dog will receive. All of these things play a part in the dog's understanding of his place in your family. You must make the commitment to give some of your time to your dog each day.

When viewing the litter as a whole, those dogs that are outgoing and seem to be in charge tend to fall into the dominant category and will generally be the leaders. Dogs that fall into this category are generally very strong-willed, and you must take charge of them. This can be a desirable trait if the dog is to be used for guarding or personal protection. Care should be taken around small children until the dog has been trained. Because of the child's smaller stature, the dog will attempt to achieve a dominant position over the child and his rightful place in the pecking order. Dogs from this category are often misunderstood. They are chosen because of their outward personality; then, when they demonstrate the leadership role, the owners become irritated with this action and want to reprimand them. In a pack, the dominant dog is the leader. You must teach your dog that you are the leader and that his position is a lower one, especially around children.

The dogs that seem to pack together, but are not attempting to be the boss, are less dominant. This is what I refer to as *assertive.* In other words, these dogs will not present a dominant posture, but they will not back down if confronted. I find these dogs to be the best for hunting and working. These are the alarm dogs that will bark an early warning, but not immediately bite. This attitude may change once separated from the litter. Do not take any dog with the hopes that it will change. Accept what you see and be ready to deal with that trait.

Those dogs that approach you in a submissive posture—head down; ears back; tail wagging nervously, and a semi-walking/crawling manner—will be considered submissive dogs. They may urinate or roll over on their backs when approached, or they may do all of the above. Shy dogs tend to be very fearful of anything that is new to them, and they require a great deal of work and socialization. They will make family pets if you are prepared to spend the time training them. They cannot be forced into any new situations, but must be allowed to work them out for themselves. Do not expect too much too soon from these dogs.

When you choose your pup, please do not make the decision that you are going to train this dog to become the family protector unless you have had experience in that field. If you have not, please seek the advice and assistance of a professional. There are many people bitten by their dog each year because they did not recognize the warning signs their dog was giving. Training for protection work requires a great deal of skill. Please seek professional help in this field.

In the years that I have spent working with unwanted and aggressive dogs, I have found that the shy or fearful dog is the one that will bite before the aggressive one. With an aggressive dog, you know what to expect. He gives you all of the signs as to what he intends to do. The shy, fearful dog will back away until cornered, and you do not know if it will submit or attack. A shy dog may submit initially, then strike out unexpectedly. When they do decide to bite, it is usually a very serious and vicious bite. Small children are the ones at risk. Due to their smaller stature, the dog considers them an equal and will attempt dominance over them. It also bears mentioning that when you place yourself at eye level with a dog, you have lowered your larger, more dominant stature, to one that is equal to the dog. When eye to eye with a dog, the dog considers you an equal.

As was once said to me by a longtime friend and mentor, Vernon Traxler, "Never say what your dog or child won't do; they'll make a liar out of you every time." Always use caution when introducing a new pup or dog into your family or new surroundings. Be on guard for how the dog will react, especially if it is a grown dog. You really do not know what this dog has been through, and it will need time to adjust to its new (pack) family. Do not rush the dog into training as soon as you get it home. Give it some time to adjust to the new lifestyle, smells, environment, and people. After two weeks of adjustment, you may start with training at a slow, methodical pace. A more detailed discussion is in the chapters on training your dog.

The following charts are provided to assist you in choosing the puppy that is right for you. Thanks in part to the research of William E. Campbell, <u>Behavior Problems in Dogs</u>, BehavioRx Systems Publications, and the behavior studies performed by him have made these charts possible.

The charts are divided into five sections. Each section contains an action that should be performed by you to judge the reaction of each puppy. There are eight puppy columns. If you are viewing a litter that has more than eight puppies, simply add the number of columns that are required.

Circle the letter corresponding to the action of every puppy in each of the sections. Count the number of As, Bs, Cs, and Ds for each puppy. At the end is a legend and scorecard for you to use. If a puppy has an equal number of As, Bs, Cs, or Ds, the test should be repeated for that particular puppy.

Dogs that register a higher number of As would fall into the dominant category, and will generally be the leaders (alpha). Dogs that fall into this category are generally very strong-willed, and you must take charge of them. This can be a desirable trait if the dog is to be used for guarding or personal protection. Care should be taken around small children until the dog has been trained. Because of the child's smaller stature, the dog will attempt to achieve a dominant position over the child, and his rightful place in the pecking order. Dogs from this category are often misunderstood. They are chosen because of their outward personality, then, when they demonstrate the leadership role, the owners become irritated with this action and want to reprimand them. In a pack, the dominant dog is the leader. You must teach your dog that you are the leader, and that his position is a lower one, especially around children.

Dogs in the B and C range are less dominant. Those in the B range are the ones that I like the best. This is what I refer to as assertive. In other words, these dogs will not present a dominant posture, but they will not back down if confronted. I find these dogs to be the best for hunting and working. These are the alarm dogs that will bark an early warning but not immediately bite. Those in the C range may become B range once they are separated from the litter. However, do not take any dog with the hopes that it will change. Accept what the test tells you, and be ready to deal with that trait.

The ones in the D range are usually very shy dogs. They will approach you in a submissive posture—head down, ears back, tail wagging nervously, and a semi-walking/crawling manner. They may urinate and roll over on their backs when approached, or they may do all of the above. Shy dogs tend to be very fearful of anything that is new to them, and they require a great deal of work and socialization. They will make family pets if you are prepared to spend the time training them. They cannot be forced into any new situations, but must be allowed to work them out for themselves. Do not expect too much too soon from these dogs.

The sections Loud Noise, Play Drive, and Retrieve Drive on the first selection sheet are important tests if you are looking for a working dog. These three tests will help you determine which of the puppies may be better suited for working and/or hunting.

Puppy Selection Chart #1

GROUP OBSERVATION - Observe the entire litter as a group.	1	2	3	4	5	6	7	8
Chases and bites or downs other puppy and stands over it. Aggressive toward others.	A	A	A	A	A	A	A	A
Alert to things going on around them. First to notice strangers. Runs toward them.	B	B	B	B	B	B	B	B
Aware of things going on but not the first to notice strangers. Usually the follower.	C	C	C	C	C	C	C	C
Appears unaware of what is happening. Sits alone away from the group.	D	D	D	D	D	D	D	D
WALK AWAY - Walk into area of litter and call or whistle. As puppies begin to move, walk away.								
Puppy follows or comes toward the sound.	A	A	A	A	A	A	A	A
Puppy runs around but cannot determine direction of sound.	B	B	B	B	B	B	B	B

Puppy looks around but does not move.	C	C	C	C	C	C	C	C
Puppy does not respond.	D	D	D	D	D	D	D	D

LOUD NOISE - (Individual test) Hit pot with large spoon (or) clap two boards together (or) blow a whistle.

Puppy is startled, but remains in the area.	A	A	A	A	A	A	A	A
Puppy runs away, but returns to area.	B	B	B	B	B	B	B	B
Puppy runs away, but returns cautiously when called.	C	C	C	C	C	C	C	C
Puppy runs away, hides, and will not return when called.	D	D	D	D	D	D	D	D

PLAY DRIVE - (Individual test) Swing a tennis ball on a string close to the puppy.

Puppy plays with ball, grasping it in mouth and tugging.	A	A	A	A	A	A	A	A
Puppy plays with ball, mouths and paws at ball.	B	B	B	B	B	B	B	B
Puppy paws at ball and walks away.	C	C	C	C	C	C	C	C

Puppy sniffs ball and walks away or ignores ball completely.	D	D	D	D	D	D	D	D

RETRIEVE DRIVE - (Individual test) Roll a tennis ball away from puppy.

Puppy chases after ball, picks it up and runs away with it.	A	A	A	A	A	A	A	A
Puppy chases after ball and plays with it.	B	B	B	B	B	B	B	B
Puppy chases ball, then leaves.	C	C	C	C	C	C	C	C
Puppy does not chase ball or ignores ball completely.	D	D	D	D	D	D	D	D

SCORE

A = DOMINANT	TOTAL								
B = ASSERTIVE	TOTAL								
C = RECEPTIVE	TOTAL								
D = SUBMISSIVE	TOTAL								

Puppy Selection Chart #2

SOCIAL ATTRACTION -(Individual test) Remove from litter and call puppy to you.	1	2	3	4	5	6	7	8
Puppy runs to you, tail up, jumping, biting at hands.	A	A	A	A	A	A	A	A
Puppy runs to you, tail up, paws at hands.	B	B	B	B	B	B	B	B
Puppy runs to you, tail down, rolls over.	C	C	C	C	C	C	C	C
Puppy does not come.	D	D	D	D	D	D	D	D

PETTING - (Individual test) Kneel down by pup. DO NOT RESTRAIN - Pet from head to tail - Test for 30 seconds.

Jumps, paws, and bites at hands.	A	A	A	A	A	A	A	A
Jumps and paws, licks at hands.	B	B	B	B	B	B	B	B
Rolls over and licks at hands.	C	C	C	C	C	C	C	C
Goes away and will not come back.	D	D	D	D	D	D	D	D

FOLLOW - (Individual test) With pup standing next to you - walk away.

Puppy follows, tail up, runs underfoot, bites at feet.	A	A	A	A	A	A	A	A
Puppy follows, tail up and running underfoot.	B	B	B	B	B	B	B	B
Puppy follows with coaching.	C	C	C	C	C	C	C	C
Puppy does not follow or walks away.	D	D	D	D	D	D	D	D

RESTRAINT - (Individual test) Roll pup on his back and hold down. Test for 30 seconds.

Puppy fights and bites at hand.	A	A	A	A	A	A	A	A
Puppy fights but does not bite.	B	B	B	B	B	B	B	B
Puppy fights momentarily then settles down. May lick at hand.	C	C	C	C	C	C	C	C
Does not fight and lick at hands. May leave after contact.	D	D	D	D	D	D	D	D

ELEVATION - (Individual test) Pick puppy up from middle of body and hold off the ground - Test for 30 seconds.								
Fights to get down, growls or bites at hands.	A	A	A	A	A	A	A	A
Fights momentarily then settles down, licks at hands.	B	B	B	B	B	B	B	B
Fights to get down, no growling or biting.	C	C	C	C	C	C	C	C
Does not struggle, may lick at hands.	D	D	D	D	D	D	D	D

SCORE

A = DOMINANT	TOTAL								
B = ASSERTIVE	TOTAL								
C = RECEPTIVE	TOTAL								
D = SUBMISSIVE	TOTAL								

When you choose your pup, please do not make the decision that you are going to train this dog to become the family protector unless you have had experience in that field. If you have not, please seek the advice and assistance of a professional. There are many people bitten by their dog each year, because they did not recognize the warning signs their dog was giving them. Training for protection work requires a great deal of skill. Please seek professional help in this field.

Chapter 2
Stages of Life

There will be periods when you will think your dog is making plans to ruin your day or that he is just trying to drive you crazy. Since dogs cannot communicate with us verbally, you should be aware of some of the things to expect as your dog ages.

As in humans, dogs will experience changes in their physical, mental, and hormonal attributes, and like humans, will react to them differently. These changes occur at various periods of their life, and if you are aware of what to expect, you will be better prepared to handle them when they happen. They experience teething, physical and mental growth, varying activity levels, heat cycles, anger, pain, the want or need to breed, boredom, contentment, discontentment, hunger and thirst, and unlike their human counterpart, never complain about it, but will seek out a means of easing these changes. Your knowledge of these changes, and when they occur, will better aid you in understanding your dog. The difference between humans and dogs is that the dog will experience these changes at a much faster rate than we do. There will be times when your patience will be tested to its limit, and you may wonder why you ever wanted a dog, but remain patient. Most problems will pass as the dog matures and with proper training.

Before outlining the stages of life, I would like to dispel the belief that a dog ages seven years for every human year. In reality, most dogs will reach the human age of twenty-one in its first year of life. Then it will gain four years for every year thereafter. The reason for the seven-to-one ratio is due to comparing the average lifespan of humans to the average lifespan of a dog. When those totals are compared, the ratio is seven to one. Knowing this may help you to understand and better cope with your dog as he matures.

Birth to Fourteen Days

During this period, a puppy is totally dependent on its mother. Puppies are born deaf and blind, so the sense of smell is paramount. The only thing a puppy is aware of at this time is where its mother is located and how to get milk from her. It cannot relieve itself without being stimulated. This stimulation is in the form of licking, which it receives from the dam. It cannot see, hear, stand, or walk, but it can crawl in a forward direction only. Puppies at this age are very susceptible to temperature changes. Since they cannot shiver at this time, it is best to keep the temperature in the whelping area around eighty degrees. Shivering creates "goose bumps," which traps warm air between the bumps. Puppies will pile on top of each other, in an attempt to regulate their level of warmth. This is "puppy ball" often seen in the whelping box.

Fourteen to Twenty-one Days

At fourteen days of age, the ear canals begin opening, and the puppy is able to hear muffled sounds. For breeds that are prone to experience deafness, this is a good time to have the hearing tested. Tests may be performed by veterinarians or veterinary schools utilizing the Baer Test. This is a procedure utilizing a computer program and electrodes connected to the exterior of the puppy's ears and head, whereby high-pitched clicking tones are sent through the connections to determine the hearing level.

The eyes begin to open, and the pupils will respond to light; however, they cannot focus or follow movement. It will take only a few more days before the puppy is able to focus on objects, and be startled by sudden movements.

This is also the period where they will attempt standing and walking. Although their attempts at walking are more of a forward stumble and fall, once accomplished, they would prefer to stand, walk, stumble, and fall than ever have to crawl again.

Teeth are beginning to break through the gums, and they will test them on each other and any other object that can be reached, including human hands.

At twenty days of age, the ears are completely open, and a puppy can hear sounds much more clearly, and is startled by loud noises. They may not be able to determine the direction of sound, but will respond readily to it.

Three to Seven Weeks

At three weeks of age, the puppy is able to eat a more solid diet of soft foods, but will still nurse on the dam. Stimulation of the bowels is no longer needed, but the dam will continue to clean up after the puppies by eating the feces, in an effort to teach them to keep their sleeping quarters clean. Chewing, playing, fighting, and posturing are now a part of their everyday activity, and they will try out their newly learned experiences on each other. Growling can be heard during play periods, which may become a lower and louder growl, implying that the play has gone too far. This is a warning that will escalate into short fights that end with one standing over the other in a dominant position. Submitting to an aggressor will end a fight, and the victor will walk away, leaving them alone.

Between five and seven weeks of age, the dam will discipline a puppy for biting or attacking her. A lot can be learned from paying close attention to the manner in which she disciplines. The dam will scold or warn a puppy with a low growl. Next, she will assume an almost upright position so that she is taller, and the growl may become more intense to make the pup understand that she means business. If the puppy's action does not stop, she will nip or shake the pup by the fleshy part on the back of his neck, known as the nape. The puppy will squeal and run to hide in the farthest corner and whimper. It should be noted that the discipline of the dam is direct, to the point, and over in an instant. It lasts no longer than the tick of a clock. The squealing and whimpering are usually out of fear and not pain. The nip that was given is nothing more than a pinch, and does not leave any marks. The dam will not go to the pup, but when the pup returns, and is behaving itself, the dam will lick the pup as a sign of her approval.

Through this observation, we learn that discipline is an important part of the learning and training experience. It should not be brutal, but it must be performed in a way that is swift, attention-getting, and establishes the leadership position. Afterward, a display of affection gives praise for a properly learned lesson.

Eight to Twelve Weeks

Most puppies will go to their new home at about eight weeks of age. Owners should allow the puppy approximately two weeks to adjust to his new surroundings, including the new people who want to play with and pet him all the time. Small corrections for biting may be made, but nothing too harsh. This is the time when most owners make serious mistakes. Between eight and ten weeks is a period commonly referred to as the "fear imprint cycle." During this period, a puppy should not be placed in any situation or training that could cause trauma or stress. Housebreaking may be taught, but it should not include any form of physical punishment. Patience is paramount at this time. (See *Housetraining* in the Problem-solving chapter.)

Socializing should begin early in the puppy's life, but not until he has received all of his vaccinations and is protected from diseases. Do not bring your new puppy to shopping centers, malls, pet stores, etc.

Keep your puppy away from locations where there may be a great deal of people and/or animals. This could be too much for a young puppy, and a number of diseases are transmitted via the air and on the clothes and shoes of people. There will be plenty of time to show off your new puppy later, when he may be more responsive to meeting other people and pets, and less likely to be traumatized.

He is in a new environment and he is learning. Let him learn how to deal with various problems on his own. Any training performed at this time should be in a positive manner and without harsh corrections. Although the dam corrected the pup in a harsh manner, as previously explained, the pup was familiar with the dam, whereas you are new to the pup and he does not know you. The pup not only has a new environment, he has lost the comfort and smells of his mother and his littermates. He knew his mother, and what was expected from her and the others in his litter. You are his new family, and he must learn all over again. Go slowly during this period, and you will be rewarded in the future. Whatever fear is placed in a pup at this time may prove to be permanent. It is very hard to turn a pup around after being traumatized.

Once brought into its new home or kennel, the pup should remain in that location. Allow him the comfort of having a place of his own, and avoid moving him repeatedly from one place to another. Whether you brought your puppy home at six or eight weeks of age, you should have one location for the pup to live for the next four to six weeks.

Except for regular veterinary visits, a puppy should not be brought into an environment outside of his living area. A puppy can be exposed to a number of diseases and parasites, both within and outside of his living area. Because of these diseases, the puppy should receive vaccinations at three-week intervals to help protect him. Your visit to the veterinarian should be handled as calmly and quietly as possible. Make it a fun trip for the puppy. While in the waiting room of the veterinarian's office, you should keep your puppy away from the other animals. You do not know the purpose of their visit or what disease may have been carried in with them. Do not force the puppy into any undesirable, frightening, or stressful situations.

Surgery at this time could be very traumatic to a puppy. Unless surgery is required to protect the puppy's life, it should be postponed to a later date. Some owners like the look of erect ears on certain breeds, and the only way to achieve that look is to crop the ears. Most veterinarians prefer to do ear cropping between ten and twelve weeks of age. It involves the removal of the leathery portion of the ear and cutting some of the cartilage. The ears are then stitched, bandaged, and set within a bracket to assist in the retention of upright ears. The reason for ear cropping is strictly cosmetic. The majority of the veterinarians I have interviewed believe the puppy will not suffer any trauma, because it is anesthetized and unaware of what is happening. I have mixed feelings about this procedure. I understand that this is the best time to perform this procedure in order to obtain a desirable result, but I am still concerned because it lies so marginally close to the fear imprint period.

At twelve weeks of age, your puppy should be nearing the end of its series of shots and should be better protected. Now is a good time to start puppy training classes and to take your puppy out into public areas for more socialization. Meeting new people and new things is very helpful in training your puppy.

Three to Four Months

The puppy begins testing everyone around it, as well as the owner's leadership. The test will begin with mouthing the hands. All too often, I hear the same complaint: "He likes to bite at my hands, but he doesn't bite hard. I know he is only playing, but his teeth are sharp. He doesn't realize he is hurting me." A truer observation would be: "He likes to bite at my hands, because they fit in his mouth. He is testing for my reaction. He is testing my leadership role, and he is looking for a response when pain is inflicted. He wants to be in charge."

All biting, mouthing, and tug of war should be discouraged. Tug of war is the agitator's tool, and is a method used to strengthen jaws, teeth, and the muscles used in fighting and biting. It is better to offer hard chew toys at this chewing stage.

Four to Eight Months

Welcome to the rebellious teenager. This is the time when your wonderful pup, that always listened and came when he was called, decides that you are not the only interesting thing around. He wants to investigate new things that you do not know about and cannot smell.

When you call him, he may start toward you, stop, and decide that a good game of chase is in order. You make a move toward him, but he runs away. You yell at him, but he stops, looks, and waits for you to run again—and you do. The pup thinks that all that yelling is your way of howling or barking, and he continues with the chase. Boy, what a fun game for the pup! Boy, are you mad!

When the pup finally decides that it is time to see what you want, you should discipline him for running away, right? Wrong! You should never discipline your pup for coming to you. Anytime you call your pup and he comes, you should praise him for coming. You want him to understand that anytime you call him, he will be rewarded with praise for coming. Coming to you should be the most pleasant experience for any dog. If you discipline him after calling him, he gets the idea that calling is the first step to being punished, and he will not want to come to you. Now is the time to begin formally training your dog, if you have not already started.

Eight to Fourteen Months

The following information is based on an average-sized dog. Some smaller breeds will mature earlier, and the larger and giant breeds will mature later.

Sexual maturity is beginning to occur, and confusion is taking place. The once-brazen dog will become wary of strangers. He will not be sure of the new things you have brought him. He will test everything slowly and hold back in situations where he used to run in to investigate. Do not despair. This is a normal reaction to becoming an adult. Being cautious is not a bad thing.

Remember when you were younger? You would run to play ball or get involved in games with others. As an adult, you are more cautious, and so is your dog. He is maturing, and he wants to be sure of what he is doing and what is going on around him. Do not force your dog into any situations that appear fearful to him. Let him work them out. Do not console your dog during these fearful moments. Most people will pet their dog and say, "It's okay; there's nothing here that can hurt you." Those soothing tones and pats are giving the signal that it is okay to be scared. Placing your hands on your dog is your sign of approval. Do not pet. Do not talk. Let him work out the problem. It will go slowly, but it will be better for him and for you in the end.

One to Five Years

Your dog will reach his physical maturity between eighteen months and two years. Although it sexually matured earlier, it will continue its growth patterns into a fully grown dog. Your dog will be sure of himself and his surroundings. He will still attempt to be in charge from time to time by testing you. He wants to see if you have become a weak leader and if you will present him with the opportunity to take charge. Since you have trained your dog by now, it is wise to work with him on his routine at least once or twice a week as a reminder that you are still in charge. Periodic training will remedy most problems that occur after maturity.

A mature dog will begin seeking out a mate. This is the ideal period for breeding. The development of testicles in the male has reached its precise levels, and the ovaries of the female should be fully functional at this time.

If breeding is not an option, you should be aware that intact males, and some dominant females, will attempt to mount whatever pleases them, including a human leg. If the mounting is problematic, then the dog should be spayed or neutered. Mounting is a hormonal function that can be discouraged by spaying or neutering.

A mature dog will mount a human in an attempt to display dominance. Even a dog that has been spayed or neutered may attempt to mount a human's leg in an attempt to present dominance over that human. Once spayed or neutered, the dog must undergo training to avoid such behavior.

Six to Ten Years

Your dog will still engage in its regular activities, but it will begin moving and running at a slower pace than it did before. It may begin to show slight graying around the muzzle and eyes.

At eight years, many dogs have a reduced appetite, and they will no longer have a need for a high-protein diet. They will begin to show signs of tiring faster, and enjoy more time resting. They will still want to do all the things they did previously, but they will not have the stamina to do them with the vigor they previously displayed.

There should be some type of activity or training to help maintain conditioning. Exercise is very important at this stage. Dogs that are allowed to lie around without any exercise will generally begin gaining weight. Weight gain is a problem for dogs as well as humans. In comparison to humans, the dog at age six is actually forty-one, and at age ten is fifty-seven years old. People slow down at this time in life, and the dog will do the same. A lack of activity and a steady diet all contribute to obesity. Exercise your dog.

At ten years, most dogs will be losing some teeth, and softer foods may be required to maintain good health. Monitoring of their food becomes necessary. They no longer need the high protein and fat formulas, but should be changed to a more maintenance or senior type of food. The amount of food may also need to be reduced. Although it sounds a bit bizarre, monitoring their stool is a means of telling if the food is being digested properly. Their stool should be firm but spongy.

Beyond Ten Years

Just like people, each dog is an individual. Some dogs may remain active for a few more years and surprise everyone around them. Others will just want to sit back, watch life, and enjoy its memories. Some will become grouchy or fussy, while others will try to continue with the pleasures they knew earlier in life. It is only a guess as to how each dog will react as it gets older.

It should be noted that, as a dog ages, life is not the same as it was earlier. We try to place on our dogs the same feelings that we place on people. It may sound harsh, but once medical help has been exhausted, euthanasia may be best for a dog that cannot embrace life as it once did. If left in the wild, or if part of a pack, the older, debilitated dog would wander away to die. Since our domestic dogs cannot escape our barriers, they are forced to live in a way that they normally would not accept.

After twelve years of age, some dogs will begin to lose sight and hearing. You will notice a considerable reduction of running activities. This is a good indication that their sight is becoming weaker. As their sight diminishes, they will have trouble getting around objects and will begin to bump into objects. As it becomes harder for the dog to hear, he may begin moving his head from side to side, trying to catch sounds. In some dogs, the loss of these faculties will cause anxiety. They will stop what they are doing and howl for no apparent reason. You may talk to them and pet them, and they will quiet down while you are there, but minutes after you leave, they begin to howl again. Most people think that the dog is just lonely, but he is suffering from anxiety. Howling is one of the means a dog will use to relieve his anxiety.

Canine cognitive dysfunction may also be the cause of behavior changes in your dog. In addition to the above symptoms, they may not recognize their owners or their surroundings. This is very similar in nature to senility in human beings.

When you see the signs of constant anxiety, trouble getting up from a resting place, the need of assistance to relieve itself of normal body functions, or any other debilitating problems, you should consult your veterinarian to determine if the problem is treatable. If treatment is not possible, it may be time to consider saying good-bye to your old friend and letting go. This letting go is hard, but it is the very best thing you can do for your dog. This is truly an act of love. Letting him suffer needlessly is a selfish act.

Saying Good-bye

I would like to tell you a short story of a great dog named Sergeant, who lived to be fifteen years old. Trained to search out and bay wild hogs and deer for his owner/trainer, Sergeant could tell when it was time to hunt just by the change in the weather. This wonderful dog would hunt on his own if he became bored. He knew that when the truck was being loaded, it was time for the hunt. He would get in the way by leaping into the back of the pickup, jumping around and barking, as if to say, "Hurry up, we're going to miss them." Amazing as it may sound, he also herded cattle with the same enthusiasm. On the hunt, he was relentless. He would not stop until the hunters were satisfied with the hunt. He could understand whether they wanted him to hunt hogs or deer. Whatever it was, they would have to call him off in order to go home. If they did not, he would stay and work until he could not go anymore.

At night, he would rest at the feet of those around him, looking for a pat on the head and maybe a little of that thing you killed. You know, just in case you had too much. As you can well imagine, all who were exposed to him loved this dog. When his owner could not hunt any longer because of his health, he would lend Sergeant to a few of his closest friends.

Even at fourteen years of age, Sergeant—without many teeth left—would want to work those hogs and cattle. Everyone knew he could not work any longer, so they would just set him up to play. This worked out great, because he thought all the while that he was still working.

At the age of fifteen, it was obvious that Sergeant could not get around or enjoy himself as he did when he was younger. It became harder and harder for him to get up, and he tired more rapidly than ever before. His impaired walk and stumble became more and more visible. Finally, the decision was made to have him put to sleep.

When the time came for Sergeant to be brought to the vet's office, only his owner, who had loved him for so many years, was in attendance. This was the way he wanted it. As the solution was administered, his owner, through watery eyes, talked to Sergeant, telling him what a great dog he had been. Sergeant looked at him as if to say, "Thank you," and passed away.

This true story was written through teary eyes, but I want you to understand that this is an act of kindness and love. It was hard for a good man to show this caliber of love for such a great and loyal dog, but he did the right thing.

Sergeant's genes live on today in my kennel, and every now and then I look in the eyes of my big male, and I swear I see Sergeant looking back.

Chapter 3
Where to Keep Your Dog

Before you can bring that puppy home, you have another decision to make. Where will your new addition sleep, and where will he spend his waking hours? Keep in mind that your puppy will not always be that little bundle of fluff that you are bringing home. He is going to grow, and he will need another, larger place when he is grown. Dogs have been kept in homes, special rooms within the home, crates, kennels, and sometimes in the back yard.

Before we get too deep into housing your dog, I want to make it clear that chaining a dog to a tree without ever giving him any exercise away from that tree can be an act of cruelty. The dog may not show any outward signs of stress, but I assure you, he is enduring it. Chaining a dog to a tree limits his ability to investigate his surroundings, mark his territory, and defend himself. Besides the frustration that will build up in him, it could cause damage to his neck and shoulders from always pulling on the end of the chain. Do not tie your dog to a tree and forget him. There are other methods of keeping your dog in a safe area without tying him down.

Some dogs will adapt to being tied or chained to a tree, but I have found that most of these dogs are there only for a short while. The owners tend to the needs of the dog, and allow them time off that chain to run and play. They get the chance to examine and explore the rest of their surroundings.

A dog wants to be with you to enjoy your company and not be tied or chained to a tree. Tying or chaining is another form of isolation. Do not isolate your dog.

If it is your intention to keep your dog in a yard, ensure that he has enough room to get some running exercises, and a boundary to keep him safe from harm and trouble. That area should be fenced off so that nothing can get in, and he cannot get out.

Many owners have invested in underground or invisible fencing. This may work to keep your dog inside a boundary, but it will not keep others out. Any dog that is placed in a boundary by invisible fencing must be trained to that fence. I've seen too many dogs run through the barrier, go off into the neighborhood, and then return home to sit outside their area waiting for the fence to be turned off. Invisible fencing works, but not as well as a physical one.

Running freely around the neighborhood is not only infringing on your neighbors, it is illegal. There have been countless disputes over roaming dogs throughout the years. Leash laws are enacted to prevent this from happening, but there are some dog owners who do not comply with that law. Then, when the dog is picked up and taken into the pound, the owners cannot understand why they have to pay to get it out.

Dogs that are allowed to roam about without any supervision tend to become very defensive and protective of what they perceive as their territory. They adopt rules of their own and begin relying on instinct to get them through the day. Then, when the dog confronts an unsuspecting child or adult, there is the problem of someone being bitten. "He's never done that before" is heard every day, and it is usually after someone has been bitten. The dog believes he has defended his space, but people do not take the time to try to understand the position the dog has taken. This leads to the possibility of the dog's life ending and the owner being fined or sued.

Keep your dog at home and in a safe area. He will need enough area that he can open up all the stops and get up a good head of steam for running. Keeping a dog confined in a yard where he cannot run will require your taking him out for that run. You may think you are taking him for a walk, but he has been walking around all day and now wants to run. You want a leisurely stroll, and he wants to run. He will need a good long walk or an area where he can safely exhaust some of that pent-up energy. This is the problem with dogs that are kept indoors. They must be exercised daily, rain or shine.

In our modern, convenient, sedentary lifestyles, we have become very haphazard about exercise. Your dog has not. He knows what he needs, and he will get it with or without you. Give him the freedom to run without danger of harm to him or others, and, if possible, get out and run with him. At the very least, take him for that long walk. I know, you are tired from all that work you've been doing, but your dog is not. He really needs the attention, and the walk or run for that required exercise is one way of giving it to him. It may even benefit you.

Sleeping Quarters (Outdoors)

Your dog will require a house that is large enough to accommodate his size and provide shelter from the weather. It should be arranged so that he can stay warm in winter and provide shelter from the rain. The house should be 50 percent longer and taller than he measures.

Example: The dog measures twenty-four inches at the withers and thirty-two inches long. This dog's house should measure thirty-two inches in height, and forty-eight inches wall to wall. This may sound a bit extreme, but if he is going to be in this house for any length of time, he will need room to stand up and turn around, and change position when sleeping. You never know how long it will be raining, and he may have to stay in his house.

I would also like to recommend that if you intend to build a house for your dog that the door be offset, either to the left or right. Do not place the doorway directly in the middle of the house. Offsetting the door will provide dead air space within the house, where the dog will be able to get away from the drafts blowing into the house. With a door situated in the center, there is no dead air space, and no shelter from the wind or drafts.

If you intend to have him come indoors at night, he will still need a place during the day. Unless you intend to be at home forever, you will have to provide him quarters outdoors. In addition, he must have plenty of drinking water at his disposal. He should not be made to wait until you want to let him back into your house before he can get a drink. Water must be made available to him while he is outdoors.

It is a good idea to have two or three toys for him to play with while he is outdoors. Dogs will become bored very easily, and destructive behavior can begin. Providing him with a few things to occupy his mind and energy level will reduce that possibility. But do not burden your dog with lots of toys. Too many toys are the same as none. He will not be able to decide which he should be playing with, and boredom will set in.

Sleeping Quarters (Indoors)

The dog that lives indoors or is brought indoors at night should have a safe area where he can sleep. This can be a crate, a room, or the garage, but he must have a place designated specifically for him. This is his safe haven where he will sleep and be out of your way if necessary. He should not be allowed free access to the whole house, except in your presence. This rule holds true for a dog of any age.

Crate training is one of the better methods for indoor dogs. This gives the dog a place where he can go and still feel safe. Dogs are den animals, and this would serve as his den. It is for him and no one else. If an open type all-wire crate is used, I would recommend covering it with a sheet or blanket. Cover all sides except the door area. This will give the dog the security he needs to know that his den is safe from attacks, and he only has to watch the entrance (door).

The crate is his safe haven, and should never be used to punish the dog. Doing so will only lead to confusion, and he will be reluctant to use the crate.

The statement that I hear about dogs indoors is this: "I let my dog roam the entire house when he is in so that he can protect me." Roaming the house while you are there is okay, but the dog must know his boundaries. When you are not at home, your dog should be in his crate or the place you have established as his sleeping quarters.

If you want your dog to protect your home, keep him outside, where he will be seen. Statistically, those wanting to enter a house to do harm or steal will avoid a house that has a dog. They do not want to be bothered with having to deal with the dog. They want to get in and out as quickly and quietly as possible. During the Sharon Tate murder case, one of the suspects was brought back to the Tate home. On his arrival, two dogs met him at the gate. The suspect stated that, had those dogs been there the night they did their deed, they would have chosen another house. Just the mere presence of a dog is enough to deter most intruders. A barking dog will attract more attention than anyone will ever want.

The major problems with indoor dogs, once housebroken, are the control of odor, hair, fleas, and chewing. The indoor dog will need some specific care to keep him clean and sweet-smelling. Flea shampoos are designed to keep fleas off your pet. You must be careful when bathing your dog that he is not bathed so often as to remove the oils from his coat. The chemicals contained in these types of shampoos could cause some problems for your dog. You can overdo the washing habit and create skin and health problems. There are shampoos designed to fight odor, but these also contain chemicals for the odor-fighting effect. It is advisable to get some guidance from your veterinarian or a qualified professional groomer before using too many chemicals on your dog. Brushing is one of the best ways to combat a good majority of these problems. Frequent brushing will keep the flea population down, remove unwanted hair, and reduce your dog's scratching. Brushing also will help relieve some of the itch associated with dry skin. The problems associated with chewing furniture and such are due to boredom or lack of exercise. Give your dog a toy or two, and exercise him regularly. This should cut down on any chewing problems.

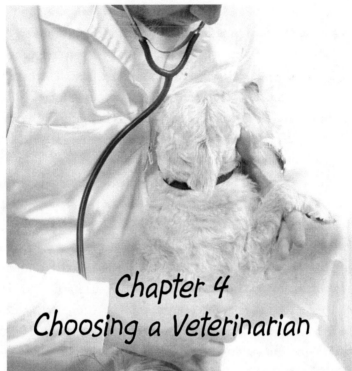

Chapter 4
Choosing a Veterinarian

More often than not, people will choose a doctor for their own health care from the phone book at a time when they are in need of immediate care. Unfortunately, pet owners will choose a veterinarian in the same manner. This is not the best time to be making choices for your care or that of your dog. It is better to plan ahead and meet with these professionals prior to requiring their services.

Before relying on the phone book to make your choice, ask your neighbors or other pet owners for the name of a veterinarian that they would recommend, and where they are located. Although location can be convenient, it should not be the only reason for choosing your veterinarian.

When you have the names of a few veterinarians, call their offices and inquire if they are a specialist or general practitioner. Do you need to schedule an appointment for your pet? Are walk-ins accepted? Do you need to pay for an appointment to meet with the veterinarian to discuss your needs? Many veterinarians will require appointments in order to keep their practice running smoothly; however, they will accept walk-ins. Walk-ins will generally have to wait longer to see the doctor, because scheduled appointments come first. The exception to this rule is that most veterinarians will accept an emergency situation without hesitation or appointment. With this in mind, if an emergency situation ever arises where there is a veterinarian closer to you than your regular veterinarian, choose the one that is closer.

As you travel about seeking a veterinarian, you may be required to make an appointment for you to visit with him and discuss your needs, but there should not be a charge for that visit.

When you arrive at his office, observe the office staff. Are they working in a proficient manner? Do they seem to care about the job they are performing? Are they friendly and courteous? While you are waiting to see the doctor, observe the waiting room. Is it clean? Are there any foul odors? Are all animals required to be on a leash or in a crate while in the waiting room? This may seem insignificant at the time, but it is an indicator as to how the business is being run. The waiting room should be clean and odor-free. This can be a breeding ground for disease. After all, animals are being brought here for routine check-ups and illnesses. You never know what illness may be lurking in the waiting room.

When you visit with the vet, do not be intimidated by his credentials. Ask the questions you need answered. When asked a question, does he answer it so that you understand, or are his answers confusing? If you are confused by his answers at the interview stage, you will be even more confused when it comes time to answer questions about treating your pet.

Ask about costs, such as office visits, shots, and routine check-ups. Although these costs vary and are ever-changing, there should not be any hesitation in giving you a quote on the approximate cost of veterinary care. Learn the hours of operation. Are they available after hours? Do they offer a weekend service? Are there emergency numbers and/or an emergency service that is used? Obtain the names, numbers, and location of the emergency service. If you are going to be selecting a veterinarian, you will need to know what emergency service they use, so that you can compare it with the other veterinarian interviews.

How many veterinarians are in the practice? How many vet techs are employed? Are X-rays, blood work, and other diagnostics done on premises or referred to other specialists? Is there a boarding facility at the location?

View the entire facility. You want to see how the clinic is being run. Observe the operating room, kennel facility where dogs are kept for observation, boarding facility, and the grounds. Are these areas clean and well cared for? These are indicators of a well-run practice.

Above all, it must be remembered that these professionals are people, too! Personalities may conflict, and that can sometime create an unwanted tension between owner and veterinarian.

If, for any reason, you feel uncomfortable with your veterinarian, you should find another. Although they may be prescribing the proper care for your dog, you may feel they are lacking in performance, based on your dislike of them. The only one that suffers here is your dog.

It is best to choose a veterinarian you feel comfortable being around and who provides the proper care for your dog, rather than to disregard good advice because your personalities get in the way. Do not allow convenience, cost, or location to be your only criteria for choosing your veterinarian.

If you leave his office not understanding what is required, one of two things happened: Either you did not ask the questions needed to acquire the answers or you did not understand the answers you received. If you do not understand the answers to your questions, let the veterinarian know. I am sure he will take the time to help you understand. It is no different than going to a pediatrician with your child. You would not leave the office without an understanding of what needs to be done or what is happening with your child. Don't leave the veterinarian's office with unanswered questions. If you think of anything that you wanted to ask, are not sure of, or may have forgotten, you should call him.

You should know the office hours of your veterinarian and be aware of the emergency telephone numbers. Your veterinarian may not always be available in emergency situations, so get to know the emergency veterinarians and their locations. Most people do not take the time to find out about who is available or where to go in an emergency until it occurs. In an emergency, time is your most important factor. Why waste that time trying to find out what to do? You should know where to go and whom you will be seeing. I have found that trying to get information on where to go and what to do in an emergency only adds to the frustration and panic. Then, when you finally get to the location, you are not happy with the way you were treated. This may not be because of the services, but because you did not know the people or they didn't talk in the same manner as your veterinarian. Take the time to learn about emergency visits before they occur. It does not take long, and you will be much happier if you know them before you use them; then, if they are needed, you will be thankful that you did.

Take this example and keep it in mind: A young woman, we'll call her Sally, and her two-year-old golden retriever were out for a walk along a country road when suddenly her dog started barking at something on the side of the road. Sally could not see what all the fuss was about because of the tall grass. As she approached, she saw a snake coiled up in the grass. She tried calling her dog to her, but the curiosity of that strange animal kept her dog from obeying her calls. Being afraid of snakes, Sally tried to retrieve her dog without getting too close to the snake. As she began to close the distance between her and the dog, she saw the snake strike. Her dog let out a yelp, jumped back, barked, and then came to her. The snake had bitten her dog.

Immediately, she placed her lead on her dog and began hurrying back to the place where she had parked her car. Not wanting to delay any attention to her pet, she drove directly to her veterinarian's office, only to find that they were closed on Sunday. She then drove home and began looking through the telephone book for the home number of her veterinarian. Unfortunately, his number was not listed. Now in a panic, she began calling other veterinarians in the area. As she called, one after another, all she would get was a recording. Without listening to the entire recording, she would hang up and dial another.

Time was passing, and her panic became worse. She decided to call a friend who had dogs and ask them what she should do. When she reached them, they directed her to the emergency number for off-hours. She made the call, and they told her to calm down and bring the dog to them.

This was a new place for her, and having never been there before, it took a little more time to locate the hospital. Once she had gotten into the parking area, she could not seem to move fast enough getting her beloved pet out of the car. It seemed as if she were moving in slow motion.

Finally, they were inside, and the veterinarian took her and the dog into the examination room. The dog was examined, given a shot, and sent home with some oral medication. Sally was told to observe her pet and call in any sudden changes. She would have to see her own veterinarian the next day.

Luckily, dogs handle snakebites much better than their human counterparts do. The dog survived the bite, but we almost lost Sally to panic and anxiety. Had Sally taken the time to talk to her veterinarian, become knowledgeable about off-duty hours, had the emergency number available, or paid a visit to the emergency location, she would have saved an enormous amount of time and anxiety. Before you are placed in a situation like this, prepare for emergencies. Do not be caught in a panic like Sally. You will be thankful that you did.

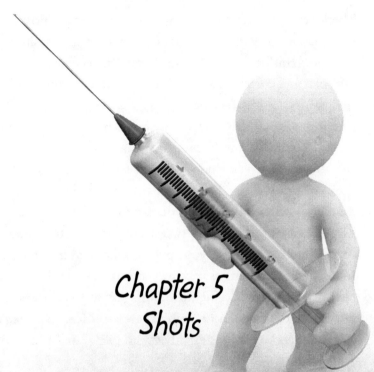

Chapter 5
Shots

I have dedicated this chapter to vaccinations and why they are needed. I wanted you to have a ready reference where you could look up the schedule of required shots. These shots are not meant to keep you going back to the veterinarian's office so that he can make lots of money. They are meant to protect you, your dog, and the public. Some of these shots are required by law in most states. If you do not comply with these laws, you could lose your dog and face penalties that are prescribed by your local agencies.

At six weeks of age, your puppy is still protected by some of the antibodies supplied by the colostrum contained in the milk it received from its mother. At this time, it should be given a vaccine containing antibodies to protect it against canine distemper, parainfluenza, leptospirosis, adenovirus 1 and 2 (hepatitis), parvovirus and coronavirus. This single shot is commonly referred to as an eight-way vaccine that primes the immune system and provides some protection against all of the above-mentioned diseases in the form of one vaccination.

There are a few veterinarians who consider the leptospirosis and coronavirus vaccine too stressful to be given to a puppy at this time, and may withhold this portion of the shot until the second visit. When the leptospirosis and coronavirus solutions are withheld, the vaccination is referred to as a six-way vaccine.

At nine weeks of age, your puppy should be given the second series of shots. This shot will include the leptospirosis and coronavirus vaccine. It, too, may be included into one single shot, which is referred to as an eight-way shot. The coronavirus vaccine may also be given independently of the others. In order for this vaccine to be effective, it must be administered twice, approximately two to three weeks apart.

At twelve weeks of age, your puppy will be given the third series of shots. If the coronavirus vaccine was not given at nine weeks, your dog will be given this vaccine now and again at sixteen weeks. Your puppy may also be given its first rabies vaccine. Most states require the rabies vaccine to be administered between twelve and fourteen weeks of age.

At sixteen weeks of age, your puppy will be given its fourth and final series of shots. The fourth shot is very important for the protection of your dog. At sixteen weeks, the colostrum that helped to protect the puppy has now disappeared from his system.

Once the vaccination program is completed, your dog will require an annual booster shot of these vaccines and a rabies booster for continued protection. This amounts to two shots in one visit. The small amount of time and money required to administer these shots is worth it for the protection of your pet.

There are other vaccines to protect your dog against Lyme disease and bordetella (kennel cough). The vaccine for Lyme disease should be given if your dog is going to be in an area where it will come in contact with wildlife. Lyme disease is carried in the deer tick and a few other species of ticks. Lyme disease can be a very debilitating disease, not only to the dog but to humans as well. The vaccine for Lyme disease should not be administered to a puppy less than twelve weeks of age. Bordetella should be administered if you intend to board your dog in a boarding kennel, or if your dog is going to be around other dogs for any period of time. Bordetella may be given as early as six to eight weeks (injection) or eight weeks (intranasal) with a booster two to four weeks later. After that, it can be administered annually. Below is a schedule that you may use for reference.

6 weeks – eight-, seven-, or six-way vaccine

9 weeks - eight-way and bordetella

12 weeks - eight-way, rabies and bordetella; Lyme disease if desired

16 weeks - final distemper/parvovirus set

Annually - booster set and rabies

Most owners will just take their dogs in for shots and not know why they need them. They know the shots protect their dogs, but do not understand what they are protected against. The following is an explanation of what you could expect to see if your dog becomes infected with the disease.

Canine Distemper—This disease begins slowly with an elevated temperature that may last one to three days, then subside temporarily. When it returns, it may last for a week or more. After the initial signs, the dog may develop conjunctivitis and respiratory infection. The dog may develop twitching in the muscles, become paralyzed in the rear quarters, and convulse. When the dog reaches the convulsive state, it is normally characterized by movement of the jaws, as if the dog were chewing gum. Next, the dog will fall over on its side and move its legs as if it were running, with loss of control of its body functions. This condition may repeat itself from ten days to several months. This disease is generally fatal. If the dog recovers from the disease, it generally will have permanent neurological damage and a permanent immunity to distemper.

Parainfluenza—This is a contagious, chronic, upper respiratory disease, and presents itself as a common cold. This disease could easily contribute to tracheobronchitis (kennel cough). It is spread via the nasal discharge from sneezing and/or the touching of noses. This disease is one that is self-eliminating and will go away in five to ten days. The vaccine is used for the prevention of canine flu or tracheitis.

Leptospirosis—Also known as yellow jaundice. At the onset, the dog may show signs of weakness, weight loss, and vomiting, with an elevated temperature. Within several days, the temperature will drop, breathing will become more labored, along with noticeable depression and an unquenchable thirst. The gums and the whites of the eyes may appear yellowish. This disease is transmitted by rodents and is usually fatal within five to ten days.

Adenovirus—Also known as hepatitis. This disease varies in severity from a slight fever to fatality. Dogs will show signs of thirst, anorexia, apathy, and may have a discharge from the eyes and nose. The clotting factor in the blood will be affected, and any bleeding will become very difficult to stop.

Parvovirus—This disease generally attacks puppies between four and twelve weeks of age, but dogs of all ages may be affected. Signs are: diarrhea, lethargy, vomiting, and rapid dehydration. Dehydration is the greatest concern, so the dog may have to be placed on intravenous fluids. This disease can be fatal within two days.

Coronavirus—Signs are similar to those of parvovirus, but may attack dogs at any age beyond four weeks of age. It is a separate and individual virus. Parvovirus vaccine will not protect against coronavirus, and vice-versa. It is advisable to vaccinate for the protection against coronavirus.

Lyme Disease—This disease is carried by the deer tick and some other species of tick. Symptoms are fever and arthritis. This disease attacks the larger joints of the animal, is very painful, and may lead to chronic arthritis.

Bordetella (Kennel Cough)—This is similar in appearance to the common cold. It is usually contracted by dogs that are congregated in one area or kenneled together. It is highly contagious and passes easily from one dog to another. Symptoms are runny noses and a dry, hacking-type cough. This vaccine is recommended if you intend to board your dog, or if he is kenneled with other dogs.

When you consider the cost of treatment versus the cost of prevention, it becomes obvious that the prevention is much less expensive. Yes, you may have to make a few trips to the vet to accomplish the protection required, but it is only in the first year. In fact, if performed in a timely manner, your dog can be protected in as little as ten weeks. We are talking about five trips to your veterinarian in a two- to three-month period to protect your dog for one year. After that, it requires one trip each year to receive a booster shot and a rabies shot to protect your dog for another year. When you consider that the cost of treating your dog for parvovirus can rise into the hundreds of dollars, it becomes obvious that prevention is the better way to go.

Chapter 6
Health Care and Grooming

For me to list all the things needed to keep your dog in the best of health, it would require another book. What I have given you here are some of the common health concerns that most dog owners encounter. These are brief explanations that are aimed at helping to keep your dog in good health. There could be residual side effects that are not mentioned here, but the general information will guide you in the right direction. It is advisable that you take your dog to your veterinarian for a correct diagnosis of any situation.

WORMS

There are five types of worms that are common to all dogs. They are: roundworm, hookworm, tapeworm, whipworm, and heartworm. Some of you will say that I have left out ringworm. Ringworm is not really a worm, but a fungus.

Each worm has its own distinctive shape, characteristics, and symptoms. All are treatable and can be cured; however, if they are left untreated, all can cause death.

ROUNDWORM

Almost all puppies are born with roundworms and must be placed on a program two to three weeks after birth. If not placed on a program, their weight and growth will be affected.

This worm comes from the dormant larvae lying in the muscles of the female dog. When she becomes pregnant, the larvae become active and move into the fetus. When the puppies are born, the larvae are already in them. Within one week of birth, the larvae will travel to the intestines and mature. In its mature state, the worm will rob the puppy of the nutrition it needs.

A grown dog may become infected with roundworm by ingesting the eggs, which may be attached to grass. Once inside the dog, the eggs will hatch into larvae that will migrate to the lungs and be coughed up. When the larvae are swallowed, they will enter the small intestines and develop into the adult worm.

Signs: Infected animals will appear "pot-bellied," with large, distended stomachs, and the rest of the body appearing thin. The coat will be dull and dry. There may be diarrhea or soft stool containing excessive amounts of mucus. Dead adult worms, which have the appearance of spaghetti, may be seen in the stool. They are long, white, and round. Eggs can be detected under microscopic examination of fecal samples.

Treatment: Pyrantel or Febantel are two of the better remedies. Treatment of the puppies should begin between two and three weeks of age and be repeated seven to ten days later. The treatment is administered in accordance with body weight.

HOOKWORM

The hookworm is passed on to nursing puppies. The larvae are usually found in the colostrum of the whelping female. The adult worm will attach itself to the walls of the small intestines, where it will feed on the blood of its host. The cycle continues when the eggs are passed in the feces of infected dogs. The eggs will hatch in twenty-four to seventy-two hours in warm, moist soil, where they may be ingested, causing the cycle to begin again.

Adults may become infected via larval invasion of the skin. The larvae will travel in the bloodstream and enter the lungs, where they will be coughed up and swallowed. The larva will attach itself to the lining of the intestines by means of a hooked mouth and begin sucking blood. An infected dog will pass hookworm eggs in their feces between fifteen and twenty days after being infected.

Signs: Anemia is the most prevalent sign of hookworm. The color of your dog's gums is a good indicator of anemia. The gums of a healthy dog will be pink in color. If you were to press against healthy gums with your finger, they would turn white immediately upon release and return to a pink color within two seconds. The gums of an anemic dog will appear white in color. Pressing against the gums would not produce any noticeable change in color. Dogs and puppies will usually be thin in appearance, and most will have diarrhea. Some may have the presence of blood in their stool. Hookworms may be detected by means of microscopic examination of fecal samples.

Treatment: Hookworm is treated in the same manner as roundworm. The dosages are determined by body weight. Both hookworm and roundworm may be treated at the same time.

TAPEWORM

Flea infestations are the cause of tapeworm infections. The larvae are present in the saliva of the flea and passes to the dog when he is bitten. The larvae will travel to the dog's intestines and mature.

The tapeworm does not suck blood, but it does rob the dog of its nutrition.

Signs: Tapeworm may be seen in fresh feces. It appears as a grain of rice that will stretch itself, resembling a tape measure. The dog will have a voracious appetite and a dry, dull, shaggy coat. He may have soft stools or a mild case of diarrhea.

Treatment: Praziquantel administered according to body weight. This may be in tablet form or injection. Flea treatments for dog, yard, and home are recommended to prevent re-infestation.

WHIPWORM

The whipworm can be found in dogs that are kept in confined areas such as small dirt yards, or chained to a specific area. Infestation is established through ingestion. The larvae will travel to the small intestines, feeding until maturity. The eggs are passed in the feces and hatch in two to four weeks in a warm, moist environment. The eggs may remain viable for up to five years in warm, moist areas. The cycle takes about eleven weeks, but the larvae may remain for up to sixteen months.

Signs: Diarrhea, weight loss, and anemia. Fresh blood may be seen in feces.

Treatment: Fenbendazole. The dog must be treated for three consecutive days in order to be successful. The dog's yard and sleeping quarters will also need treating. This area should be kept clean and dry.

HEARTWORM

Mosquitoes are the carriers of this disease. Microfilaria may be found in the blood of an infected animal. Mosquitoes, feeding on an infected host, will ingest the microfilaria, which will remain in them for approximately two weeks. The larvae will travel to the mouth of the mosquito, where it will be passed on to the next host. The larvae will live in the tissue of its host for about two months. Then it will travel to the right ventricle of the heart, where it will remain, mature, and begin passing microfilaria. Adult worms may live in the heart for years, while increasing in numbers. This increase in numbers will take up space and interfere with the normal function of the heart and may cause death.

Signs: Tiring easily, falling down as if the dog were having a seizure, continuous cough as though something were caught in his throat, and visible weight loss are the more common signs.

Treatment: Two injections of Melarsamine for two consecutive days are used to kill adult heartworms. A microfilaricide should be administered within three to four weeks after the injections.

Prevention is the best treatment. Some oral preventatives must be given daily, while others are manufactured to be given monthly. Also available and very effective is a bi-annual vaccine. Three chemicals have been found to be highly effective: Ivermectin (Heartguard—monthly), milbemyain (Interceptor—monthly), and diethylcarbamazine (Filaribits—daily) are the most popular choices.

PESTS

SARCOPTIC MANGE

Sarcoptic mange is caused by a highly contagious parasitic mite. The mite goes through four stages in its cycle and takes between eighteen and twenty days to complete. All four stages are spent on the dog. The female mite will burrow under the skin of its host to lay her eggs. The dog will scratch and chew at his body in an attempt to relieve the itching sensation caused by the burrowing mite, thus creating open sores. The scratching will lead to a secondary infection. The secondary infection is usually much worse than the original problem and could cause death if untreated.

Signs: Continual scratching or chewing; hair loss; dry skin. The mite may be detected from skin scrapings viewed under a microscope.

Treatment: Anti-seborrheic or sulfur shampoo, and dipping solutions. You must first wash your dog and then apply the solution. You may dip the entire dog into the solution or you may sponge it on. In either case, allow the solution to dry on the dog. Do not towel dry.

Ivermectin given orally and measured in accordance with body weight may also be used as a treatment.

DEMODECTIC MANGE

Demodectic mange, commonly called "red mange," is also caused by mites. It is not contagious, but it is much harder to eliminate than sarcoptic mange. The mite will actually cut the hair and live in the hair follicle. The life cycle is between twenty and thirty-five days.

It is believed that all dogs have this mite, but most have immunity to some degree. This mange will usually appear in a young dog before it reaches one year of age. The symptoms will generally appear when the dog has some type of physical or psychological stress.

Signs: Small hairless patches around the eyes, on the face or neck. Small pustules resembling human pimples may also appear. This may spread over the entire body. Examining skin scrapings under a microscope is the only way to identify the demodectic mite.

Treatment: A topical application of Amitraz every two weeks until no live mites are found. More recently, the use of Ivermectin in prescribed amounts over a thirty-day period has proven effective in combating demodectic mange.

FLEAS

The flea secretes anticoagulant saliva, which enables it to feed freely on its host. The flea will continue to feed even after it is full. The continual feeding stimulates the egg-laying process. The eggs are laid and fall off the dog. When the eggs hatch, the larvae feed off the blood-rich feces of the flea until it reaches adulthood. It will then find a host, and the cycle begins again. A flea can live up to two months without feeding. Some dogs will have an allergic reaction to flea bites.

Signs: Continual scratching and chewing. There may be some hair missing from around the areas of the neck, back, or base of the tail; hot spots; black specks on the skin. If these specks turn red when placed on a wet paper towel, your dog has fleas. Even if there are no fleas visible, these black specks are flea feces and definitely indicate the presence of fleas.

Treatment: Combating fleas can be an exhausting chore. In order to be successful, you must treat the dog, its living quarters, yard, and home simultaneously. To treat one without the other is only postponing the re-appearance of this pest. The yard and the home may be treated with Fipronil (Frontline), Bifenthrin (Talstar), and a variety of pyrethroids. It is best to spray the yard every third day for nine days. This will insure killing the hatching eggs, as well as the laying fleas. Keep your dogs off of the sprayed areas until it has had a chance to dry. The dog should be washed and dipped every twenty-one days, until there is no sign of fleas.

There are topical flea-killing products that may be applied to your dog, and are available through veterinarians; however, treatment of the dog's surrounding area is still advisable.

Caution: Be extremely careful when spraying insecticides. They could be very toxic to your dog. Read all labels carefully and follow the directions explicitly. If there is no mention of dogs or fleas on the label, contact your veterinarian and ask for his advice.

TICKS

There are approximately 1,500 different species of ticks that fall into five categories. These categories are: hard, soft, leathery, poultry, and reptiles. The information on these bloodsuckers takes up sixteen pages in the *Merck Veterinarian Manual.* Since there are so many of these parasites, I will not attempt to describe them. The best that can be said is they can cause great problems if the proper action is not taken.

Ticks can be found in tall grass, trees, lumber that is stored outdoors, and just about any cool, damp area. They have a means of detecting the body temperature of the approaching host. A tick's first choice will be to attach itself to the neck and ear area of your dog. Check inside the ears, as well as the outside. Ticks seem to like the meaty portion of the interior ear. You may also find ticks in the soft areas of the legs, around the anus, the soft area of the genitals, on the tail, and between the toes and the underside of the toes. Occasionally, ticks will be found on the back or side of the dog. This will occur when the dog has become infested with them.

The best method for removing ticks is to use tweezers or one of the newer tick-removal tools on the market. The tick has a pincher-type mouth that enables him to hold on to his host. You don't want to kill the tick prior to its removal. If the tick is killed, it will not be able to release its grip. This could result in the head being left in the dog. If the head should break off and remain in the skin, it will usually become infected. This must be treated so as not to cause secondary infection or other serious problems. Grasp the body of the tick firmly and apply a steady pulling pressure until the tick releases itself. Next, medicate the injured area with alcohol.

There is proof that several species of ticks transmit Lyme disease. Lyme disease may also be contracted by humans. The tick will have to remain on its host for a period of twenty-four hours in order to pass on the disease. That is why it is so important to remove the tick as soon as possible. Also, severe tick infestation may cause anemia and death.

Anytime you or your dog are in an area where ticks may be found, you should check your dog and yourself thoroughly. Comb or brush your dog before putting him in his kennel or letting him in the house. Washing your dog with a flea-and-tick shampoo will help reduce the number of ticks your dog will attract. Be careful when washing your dog with these shampoos. Follow the directions on the label. Too much of the active ingredients could be absorbed through the skin and cause you and your dog to have a negative reaction.

There are topical repellents, available through veterinarians, which may be applied to your dog on a monthly basis. These products are very effective at repelling ticks.

EAR MITES

This little devil will cause more problems than you can imagine. The ear mite lives in the ear canal, sucking lymph by piercing the tender skin inside the ear. This will cause irritation, inflammation, and the formation of a crust. If you see your dog scratching at his ears and whining, there is probably a good reason.

Signs: The dog will shake his head frequently and scratch or rub his ears. A dark brown, waxy substance can be seen in the ears. In some cases, there may be a noticeable odor coming from the ears.

Treatment: Hold the dog so that he cannot shake his head. Place approximately 1 ml of 50 percent alcohol and white vinegar mixture in the ear. Massage the base of the ear for approximately fifteen to twenty seconds. Release the dog and allow him to shake this out. Repeat the same procedure for the other ear. Next, apply a miticide solution into each ear. Massage the ears in the same manner and hold the dog for as long as possible, so the miticide can do its job. This should be done every third day for four applications.

Prevention: Clean the dog's ears each time you clean the dog. Using a 50/50 mixture of rubbing alcohol and white vinegar to periodically clean the ears will help prevent bigger problems in the future.

DISEASES

RABIES

Rabies is transmitted by means of saliva. The disease is passed on when an infected animal bites its victim. The infected animal does not necessarily have to be another dog. It could be any number of animals. If your dog is allowed to roam the woods, or if you take it hiking and camping, it could encounter an infected animal. Because of the sniffing process used by dogs, there is a possibility that the disease could be passed on by means of inhalation. The disease could be present in the dog even if it is not showing any immediate signs of infection. The incubation period is between fifteen and fifty days.

Signs: Change in behavior; not eating or drinking; seeking isolation from everyone; frothing or drooling at the mouth.

Treatments: There is a minimally effective treatment. The dog generally dies.

Prevention: The reason for a minimal amount of rabies in the United States is due to the fact that dogs are vaccinated annually. Not getting your dog vaccinated is irresponsible and dangerous. This vaccine has been proven to prevent the spread of rabies in dogs. It is impossible to vaccinate all the animals in the wild. Because these animals in the wild cannot be vaccinated, rabies is still with us today. In addition to your dog being protected from the rabies virus, you lessen the chance of human infection. Rabies treatments for humans are available.

DISTEMPER

Distemper is a highly contagious disease closely related to measles. The virus is sensitive to disinfectants and cannot live outside the body. There is a belief that this disease may cause multiple sclerosis in humans; however; there has not been any clinical proof of this.

Signs: High fever; runny nose; reddening of the eyes; and/or convulsions; depression; diarrhea. "Chewing-gum fits," or the chopping of teeth together, will cause excessive drooling. The dog will lie on its side with the legs moving as if it were running. The dog will have no control over normal body functions. Rear muscles will twitch or fail first. Blood tests will reveal a low white blood count.

Treatment: Lots of fluids; antibiotics to prevent secondary infection; nasal spray, and anticonvulsant. Keep the dog comfortable and calm. Most infected dogs will die.

Prevention: A series of vaccinations as a puppy with an annual booster.

PARVOVIRUS

A very highly contagious disease, parvo is spread by the ingestion of fecal matter of infected animals. Dogs do not necessarily have to eat feces or urine to become infected. Since dogs seek out certain types of grass, it is possible for the matter to be on that grass. An infected dog may shed the virus for up to two weeks. The virus may remain viable for years. Although dogs of any age may acquire parvo, puppies between eight and twelve weeks of age seem to be more susceptible. Incubation of the disease is from three to eight days. Signs may not appear for as many as seven or eight days. Death may occur within twenty-four hours after the first sign. Recovery may take from two to eight days.

Signs: Diarrhea containing blood; anorexia; rapid dehydration; foul odor in feces. Some dogs may have a fever.

Treatment: Prompt, intensive care; plenty of fluids and antibiotics. Intravenous fluid therapy is highly recommended.

Prevention: A series of vaccinations as a puppy, with an annual booster vaccination.

CORONAVIRUS

Coronavirus is also a highly contagious disease. Although coronavirus is a different disease than parvovirus, it is similar in its symptoms. The treatment and prevention are the same as for parvovirus.

HEPATITIS

There are two types of hepatitis. Both types attack the liver, kidneys, and spleen. The disease is spread by the urine, feces, or saliva of infected dogs. The reactions vary from a slight fever to death. Young dogs are more at risk than older ones. The incubation period is from four to nine days. A higher than normal temperature will be observed for one to six days. The normal temperature of a healthy dog is between 101 and 102.5 degrees.

Signs: Apathy; anorexia; runny nose; watery eyes; and hemorrhaging. The clotting factor in the blood is the most affected. A small cut will bleed uncontrollably, and bleeding is possible at the gum line.

Treatment: Periodic blood transfusions, which is a very expensive process.

Prevention: A series of shots as a puppy and an annual booster.

LEPTOSPIROSIS

This disease is spread by the common brown rat. Dogs of any age are at risk. Males appear to be affected the most. Incubation is five to fifteen days. Death will occur within five to ten days.

Signs: High temperature for several days, then a sudden drop. The dog will experience labored breathing and unquenchable thirst. Deep depression; the dog does not want to rise or move about. He may suffer from sharp abdominal or back pain. Jaundice may be present, which may be seen as a yellowing of the gums and/or eyes. Blood tests will reveal a high white blood cell count.

Treatment: Penicillin followed by Tetracycline. High doses of vitamin B. Intravenous feeding may be necessary. This, too, is a very expensive process.

Prevention: A series of vaccinations as a puppy and an annual booster.

PARAINFLUENZA

Parainfluenza is another cause of kennel cough. This causes flulike symptoms.

Signs: Constant nagging cough; sneezing; and watery eyes. This is not as serious a disease as the others mentioned, but it will open the door to secondary infection. Once in the kennel, it can cause havoc. If one dog is infected, it is recommended that all dogs be treated. This disease can be transmitted from one to the other and then back again.

Treatment: May be supported by a broad-spectrum antibiotic.

Prevention: A series of vaccinations as a puppy and an annual booster.

After reading about all those shots and boosters, you are probably wondering how a dog can take all those shots. Parvovirus, coronavirus, distemper, hepatitis 1 & 2, parainfluenza, and leptospirosis vaccines are manufactured so that they can be administered in one shot. After a series of three shots at three-week intervals, starting at six weeks of age, the dog may receive one annual booster shot. It will also need an annual rabies shot.

Two shots a year will help to protect your pet. This is a lot less costly than having to treat one that is ill, and it is not as painful as having to put it to sleep due to your lack of prevention.

GENERAL INFORMATION

EARS

The ears are usually the most overlooked portion of the dog. Any dog that swims can get an infection from having water enter the ear. Dogs whose ears hang down will tend to maintain a moist area, allowing bacteria to thrive. Bacterial and/or fungal infections in the ear canal are called otitis.

Signs: The dog will continuously shake his head in an attempt to rid itself of the irritation inside.

Treatment: Clean the dog's ears with a 50/50 mixture of rubbing alcohol and white vinegar. Place approximately 1 ml of this solution in the dog's ears. Massage it in gently from behind the ears, and then clean them out with cotton balls. You cannot reach a dog's eardrums with your fingers because of the makeup of the dog's ears; however, do not attempt to go any deeper than you can see.

EYES

Dogs like to roll around in grass, sand, and mud. During this action, the dog may get some debris in its eyes. This will irritate the eyes, and, if not cared for, could cause a greater problem.

Signs: Rubbing at the eyes. A crusty buildup in the corners of the eyes may develop, or a reddening of the eyes, especially under the eyelid.

Treatment: Flush the eyes with eyewash. This will help remove any debris that may be the cause of the irritation. Next, apply an antibiotic eye ointment. Be careful with this tube around the eye. If the dog should suddenly move, it could cause a more serious injury.

TEETH

A dog's teeth are his defense system and his only means of picking up things, including food. You should check you dog's teeth regularly. Once a month, you should brush his teeth and check for decaying teeth or any problems with the gums. If your dog will not let you brush his teeth, take him to your veterinarian. If the teeth are allowed to decay, they will cause health problems for your dog. If they are not cared for properly, the gums will suffer. Food will stick between the dog's teeth just like yours. You must help him get rid of this left-behind food.

Chew toys that will allow a flossing effect are helpful, but you should have his teeth cleaned. This is just another way to add longevity to your pet's life.

FEET

The feet are another area that requires attention from time to time. Check between the toes for pests, sores, or debris that may cause irritation. Be certain to clean between the toes when bathing your dog.

Toenails should be checked regularly. Keep them neatly trimmed. Sharp nails can cause nasty cuts to a human's thin skin. If the nails are allowed to grow too long, they can become an irritant to the dog. Have your veterinarian show you how to clip your dog's toenails.

GROOMING

When grooming is mentioned to a dog owner, the first thing that often comes to mind is the amount of money it is going to take to have the dog looking good. Of course, there are professional groomers who have all of the equipment and the expertise to maintain the special look of your dog's breed. Grooming, as discussed here, is a means of keeping your dog clean, healthy, and looking nice. There is not a lot of time required to groom your dog. It is a matter of keeping up with what the dog needs to keep him looking like the special dog that he is. Here is some information that may help you keep your dog properly groomed.

Indoor dogs may be washed as often as once a week if the washing is followed by a crème rinse. This sounds like the dog is going to need beauty parlor treatments. The truth is that weekly washing may dry out a dog's skin, and he will begin scratching due to the dryness of his skin. The scratching will sometimes cause a secondary infection, and the owner will not be able to figure out why his dog is always scratching. The crème rinse will help to condition the skin and coat and prevent it from drying out, thus eliminating the scratching.

Outdoor dogs should be washed monthly. A crème rinse will also help them. Flea and tick shampoos and dips will give protection for approximately fourteen days. Continuous use of these types of shampoos could dry out the dog's skin.

Some breeds have hair that grows inside the ears. You should check for this and remove any hair inside the ear. This hair will help keep the ear moist and cause some of the problems mentioned above.

Brushing your dog should be done as follows: long-haired dogs, once a week; medium-haired dogs, every two to three weeks; short-haired dogs, once a month. The brushing should go to the skin, and not just the top coat. The way to do this is to brush the coat in sections. This may be referred to as *line brushing*. Select a section to be brushed, and brush with the grain, all the way to the skin. Take the next section and do the same thing until the entire dog is brushed.

Since you are already working with the dog, go ahead and check those toenails. They should be trimmed or filed once a month. Keeping the nails short will help prevent the dog's feet from becoming sore, and it will reduce the scratches you receive while playing with him. Ask your veterinarian for the correct procedure and tool if you have any reservations about administering this grooming step.

Yards and Kennels

The most overlooked detail by some dog owners is the removal of stool from their yard. They feel that once the dog eliminates in the yard, Mother Nature will take care of the rest. This may be true in the wild, where there are acres of land for the dog to use, but when confined to a small yard or portable kennel, the stool does not break down fast enough, and could cause some health problems for the dog and you.

When a dog lives in a kennel, its area should be cleaned twice daily to minimize its stepping in feces. In a yard, the cleaning should be done a minimum of every other day. One of the problems that can occur from improper maintenance is coprophagia, more commonly known as stool eating. Although not considered serious in itself, and viewed as disgusting to humans, it does not seem to bother the dogs or cause any immediate health issues. There are numerous explanations as to why dogs do this; however, regular removal of feces from the area will help to eliminate the problem. Besides eliminating this habit, you are also eliminating the possibilities of the dog's ingesting any bacteria that could produce greater problems for it and you.

Another problem that can be caused from leaving stool is coccidia. This bacterial infection will cause diarrhea and fluid loss in your dog. Although it is not life-threatening, treatment would require a sulfur-based medication to be given twice daily over a ten-day period to eradicate the bacteria. A thorough cleaning of the yard, sleeping quarters, food and water bowl is required to prevent re-infection.

Eliminate the possibility of your dog's getting sick from his own waste by picking it up and disposing of it. If left unattended, this could become a health issue, which could ultimately lead to legal problems in the future. Your neighbor could file a report with animal control and/ or the health department. It is not that hard to pick it up or remove it, so take the small amount of time required to do it, and eliminate any unforeseen problems.

Monthly spraying of your yard and kennel with a mixture of two cups of bleach to one gallon of water will reduce bacterial growth and provide a safe environment for you and your dog. There are some commercially made products, such as Lime, that may be used, but I find the bleach mixture to be just as effective.

LAGNIAPPE

Pronounced "lan-yap," it is a word used in Louisiana meaning "a little something extra." There are over-the-counter medications that can be used to help your dog. For example, if a bee stung your dog, you could administer one teaspoonful of an antihistamine to your dog to afford him some relief and help prevent allergic reactions. Meat tenderizers, applied wet and rubbed into insect stings, will help break down the protein in the venom, giving some relief. Eye drops may be used in your dog's eyes in the same way you use them for yourself.

There are three major points that have increased the lifespan of dogs. They are:

1. Control of infection and disease through vaccines.

2. Heartworm prevention.

3. Automobile death prevention. Both those run over by cars and those left in closed cars. Two major points to save newborn pups are:

1. Heat source. Keep your puppies warm. Prevent them from getting a chill.

2. Sugar water if they become chilled or sick. Mix one teaspoon of honey to eight ounces of water. Give 1 ml orally every thirty minutes to prevent dehydration. Pediatric electrolytes may also be used. Administer 1 ml every thirty minutes. Do not dilute. Two major points for geriatric pets are:

1. Obesity. Weigh your dog once a month to help control its weight.

2. Keep the dog's teeth clean. Remove those that are decayed. Decayed teeth can cause health problems.

Chapter 7
Food & Water

T here are almost as many brands and varieties of food available for dogs today as there are varieties and breeds of dogs. There are chunks, pellets, soft, crunchy, kibbles, high-protein, low-fat, puppy formula, adult formula, senior formula, and the list goes on. No wonder owners are confused by what they should be giving their dog.

Most dog owners are more concerned with price than any other factor. Price, at first glance, appears to be important, but I would like to show you why price should not be the only factor considered when choosing a dog food. Of course, if you can obtain a quality dog food at a reasonable price, you should take advantage of it.

Let's start with the rules of dog food. The industry standard is required by law that all dog food, canned and dry, must have an ingredients label. The first ingredient appearing on that label must be the primary ingredient. The ingredients on the label are listed in the order of their content. If you look at an ingredients label on a bag of dry dog food, and you see rice as the first ingredient, it is indicating that rice is the primary ingredient. In most of your quality dry dog foods, you will see meat, fish, poultry, or lamb as the primary ingredient. This indicates that the main source of the protein is from this ingredient.

When viewing canned foods, the first ingredient you will see is water. Most often they will read, "Enough water for cooking." If water, in any explanation, appears first inside the ingredients label, then the primary ingredient is water.

In order to understand what your dog is actually receiving from his food, you must look at the ingredients label. Here are two examples. If the label reads like this: "Ingredients: beef, rice, poultry by-products, etc.," the main ingredient is meat. If the label should read like this: "Ingredients: enough water for cooking, meat, etc.," it is telling you that the main ingredient is water.

I am not condemning canned dog foods. They have a place in the world of dog foods and can be useful in many instances. I am, however, trying to point out to you that, even though you feel you are getting a bargain, it may not be the bargain that you think you are getting.

The bargain brands of dry dog food are price-appealing, but look at the labels. On dry foods, you want to look not only at the first ingredient, but pay particular attention to the first five ingredients. The word *corn,* in any form, appearing more than once in the first five ingredients, indicates that you are probably feeding mostly corn. Corn is not very digestible for humans or animals.

When you feed your dog a good, high-quality dry dog food, he will be getting all the required nutrients he needs. The protein and fat contents are equally important. The amounts of protein and fat intake are generally determined by the age and activity level of your dog. Young, healthy, active dogs should be receiving a high-protein and -fat diet, whereas an older dog will not need the higher amounts of protein and fat, because he will not be as active as a younger dog. Your veterinarian can help you in deciding what protein and fat contents you should be feeding your dog. I prefer foods that contain 22 to 26 percent protein and 15 to 18 percent fat. In addition to putting more nutrients inside your dog, you will be picking up less waste (stool) with a quality dry food, because your dog will be using his food in a more efficient manner. More of the food will be used to benefit the dog, resulting in less output of waste. Quality dry dog foods are designed to put more nutrients into your dog with as little waste as possible.

An adult dog should relieve himself an average of twice a day. If your dog is relieving himself more than this, the protein that you think he is getting is more than likely ending up on the ground. This means that you must feed more and more food in order for him to maintain his proper weight. Along with increased feeding of this food comes increased waste. With a quality dry dog food, you will be feeding less food, maintaining a proper weight, and cleaning up less waste.

Most people do not associate the waste factor when buying dog food. If you compare the amount of food you are feeding with the amount of waste you are cleaning, you will get a better idea of how much food your dog is actually using. A good high-quality food will provide all that is needed, with less food being given and less waste to clean.

Doesn't it make sense to provide your dog with what he needs? You can make the decision on what brands of food to feed, but discuss with your veterinarian what he thinks is appropriate for your dog. Compare dog food the same way you would compare your own foods. It is as important for your dog to receive the proper nutrients as it is for you. Feeding a quality food will help make your dog happier and healthier. Remember, he cannot go shopping when he decides he would like something to fill his empty feeling, so it is up to you to get him what he needs and deserves.

Puppies between the ages of three weeks and six months should be fed two to three times a day. You must monitor the amount of food you are giving, rather than just let them have food whenever they want it. Puppies will eat almost everything you put in front of them. They do not know how to gauge the amount of food they need. This can be seen when a puppy's stomach swells after eating. It appears as if he has swallowed a balloon. It is better to give them their food and allow them fifteen minutes to eat. Most will finish eating in less time than this, but if they still have food after fifteen minutes and are not eating, pick it up. At the second and third feedings, do the same thing. Eventually you will be able to gauge the amount of food your pup requires at each feeding. You must also be aware that your pup is growing and will need gradual increases in his daily amounts.

When your puppy reaches six months of age, take him off the puppy food and place him on an adult formula. You should also begin feeding him once a day, either morning or evening, whichever is more convenient for you. The amount you feed him should be equal to the total amount of food that he was receiving in two or three feedings, but now he is receiving it in one feeding.

Controlling the food will help you to gain respect from your dog. By monitoring his intake and outflow, you have a much better idea of how your dog's system and body functions are performing from day to day.

Some veterinarians will disagree with taking the dog off puppy food at six months of age. Most want to see you feeding them puppy food until they are one year old. Now, bear with me as I stray for a moment in an attempt to explain my reasoning. The average age gain for dogs is estimated at seven dog years per one human year. This figure is the average and eliminates mathematical equations for most people. In truth, a dog reaches age twenty-one when it celebrates its first birthday. Thereafter, it gains four human years per year. This means that at six months of age, your dog is approximately twelve to fifteen years of age. Do you know any twelve- to fifteen-year-old children who are still eating baby food? So why should your dog eat puppy food? Growing bones at a rapid or accelerated rate can lead to major problems for the dog as he ages. For this reason alone, I do not recommend puppy foods beyond six months of age. A good-quality adult formula is what I recommend.

I have heard stories about dogs that would not eat because they did not like the food. This is nonsense. A dog can go three days without eating, and not experience any serious side effects. If you give him food and he does not eat it, pick it up. Give it to him again the next day. If he still does not eat, give it to him the third day. He will begin eating. The main reason dogs get their way with not eating a certain food is because people assume the dog does not like the food and they cannot accept the dog not eating. When the dog refuses to eat, they feel sorry for him and give him anything he will eat. They believe that he must have something to eat or he will become ill or starve to death. Then, when they are serving the dog what he wants, they say the dog is a finicky eater and will eat only certain things. Do not be fooled into believing this myth. A dog will not allow itself to starve to death. If he refuses to eat on the third day, he is having a problem and should be taken to your veterinarian. Do not let him fool you. He will eat on the third day, in the majority of cases.

If you decide that you must change food, or you find something that is better for your dog, do not change it immediately. Make the change gradually over the course of five days. Start off by adding some of the food you want to change to, then increase the amount of the new food and decrease the amount of the old food. This way, the dog is still eating the quantity of food it had before the change. By the end of the fifth day, the dog should be eating only the new food. This method is not to fool the dog, but to make it easier on his stomach. If you were to change from one type of food to another rapidly, it could cause your dog gastric stress, resulting in diarrhea. Normally, it would take about five days for the dog's digestive system to adjust to the rapid change in food, so why not save him the stress, and just change the food gradually?

Table food is human food. It is not meant for the dog. Dog foods contain all the protein, fat, vitamins, and minerals a dog needs. Foods that are prepared for consumption by a dog are better for him than any leftovers you can give him. Table food, fast food, prepared meals, and slaving over a stove for humans are not the foods meant for a dog. Agreed, some of the products that are in dog foods are very similar to what we eat, but the food we eat is not the nutritious diet that a dog needs. Just take a look at us humans. Do we eat all the right foods?

Do we follow the nutritional chart when preparing our own foods? Do we eat the proper amounts of those foods? The answer to these questions is "NO." Your dog can have all the right foods, in the proper amounts, prepared for his health, in one serving of dog food. Do not feed table food. Scraps are just that. Throw them away.

Doggie treats are okay once in a while, but they should not be given as a daily portion of food, a replacement for food, or a supplement to food. A treat is just a "goodie" for the good dog. Before giving your dog a treat, make him earn it. Have him sit, lie down, roll over, dance, or anything else that comes to mind. You do not have to ask much from him, but he should earn every treat he gets.

WATER

Your dog will need an ample supply of water, which should be changed daily and be readily available. Dogs may go without food for days, but they cannot go without water. Make it a point to check his water bowl/bucket, and be certain that he has a fresh and ready supply of it. Your dog is wearing his overcoat all year long, and sometimes it gets very warm for him. Water is the fastest way for him to cool himself off.

The same is equally important—if not more important—for the dog that lives outside. In the summer months, especially in the Southern states, it is advisable to check the water twice a day. Water is an excellent conductor and absorbs heat. When the bucket gets hot, the water inside heats up as well. I have seen buckets placed in shaded areas where it was thought to be cool, only to have the water become warm to the touch. If the ambient temperature is 90 degrees, the water in the bucket will eventually achieve that temperature. A warm, overheated dog does not want warm water to drink, so check and change it often.

It deserves mentioning that warm water will also assist the growth of algae. A green, slimy substance resembling someone's science project does not belong in your dog's drinking water. Cleaning the bowl/bucket with a bleach solution will aid in removing this problem.

Keep in mind that standing water that is allowed to become stagnant is a good breeding ground for mosquitoes. Mosquitoes are the central source of heartworms. Remove all standing water and keep those water buckets clean.

This may sound overly simple, but that is all there is to it.

Chapter 8
Conditioning Your Puppy

Puppies will sometimes try your patience to the very last nerve. You must keep in mind that the cute little puppy you acquired at six or eight weeks of age will remain a puppy for another eight months. Just because he has reached sexual maturity does not mean that he has reached adulthood. The differences between a young puppy and one that is six months old are the size, strength, rate of growth, and span of attention. If you have a young puppy that is going to turn into a goliath when it is full grown, do not wait until there is a struggle of wills and strength to begin training it. Start training that puppy while it is still small enough for you to handle without too many difficulties.

The most important thing to keep in mind about a puppy between eight and ten weeks of age is that you must make every effort to avoid creating any traumatic situations as seen in the eyes of the puppy. This period is referred to as the "fear imprint cycle." I have heard some owners say that this is just a means of letting a puppy get away with anything it wants. That is not true. In fact, it would be akin to having someone frighten an infant child. Anything that serves to frighten or cause the puppy to seek refuge could be imprinted on his brain for life. Included in imprinting is hitting, spanking, swatting, shaking, or any other physical correction that will cause a great amount of fear. Take it slow and calm. Keep in mind that a twelve-week-old puppy's attention span is about five minutes. Puppies are eager to learn, hungry for affection, and always curious. Use this to your advantage. Spend the time to help them learn, but use caution to prevent any situation that could be traumatic to your puppy during this period.

A number of my clients have remarked that having a puppy is like having a child. Well, that is not too far from the truth. Treat and train the puppy in the same manner as you would a child. For example: If your child were to have an accident by soiling its clothing, you would not rub his nose in it, would you? No! You would understand that this is a normal function that cannot be avoided, but it will change in time as you instruct the proper means of elimination. You may have some concern, but you would handle the situation calmly and without creating a stressful situation. Do the same with your puppy.

Here are some of the things that you should do with your puppy, while it is still a puppy. Waiting too long to begin training allows the dog to develop its own rules and habits that may be harder to change. Breaking bad habits is much more difficult than teaching new ones. Start training the puppy, and the adult that develops will know the rules, understand your authority, be more acceptable to training, and try to please you in all of its actions.

Exposure

"Hey, I just got a new puppy! Do you want to see it?"

Everyone reacts that way with his or her new addition. The only problem here is that the puppy is being exposed to an onslaught of new people, sounds, odors, and diseases. Observe how most people will pick up a puppy and hold it close to them, cuddle and reassure it, only to shove it to someone else to hold, or place it rapidly on the ground. Pay attention to the puppy's reaction. He will stretch out his paws and stiffen his body in fear. The next person who takes the puppy will reassure it with comforting words, such as, "It's okay, puppy, I'm not going to hurt you." What is not understood is that you may be hurting him in the form of trauma or disease. Keep your puppy in his new environment until he has received all of his shots. It is okay for people to visit, but some precautions should be taken until the pup is twelve weeks of age. I do not recommend taking a young puppy with you when you go shopping or visiting, until after the series of required shots and examinations have been completed. Puppies are most vulnerable to diseases at this time, and it is going through the "fear imprint cycle."

It is better to avoid strange animals or other environments, until after your puppy has received all of its shots. There are a number of diseases that can be transported on clothing or shoes simply by being in an area where a disease is present. Puppies can pick up these diseases by walking in areas where others have walked or by being held against the clothing of a person who has unknowingly come into contact with an airborne disease. As they walk around, they are spreading the disease without their knowledge. Along comes your puppy, and three to ten days later, you can't understand why your puppy is very ill. These shots will help protect him. After he has completed his series of shots, he will be better protected, and you may take him wherever you like.

When you take your puppy to the veterinarian's office for his shots, keep him close to you. Do not let him sniff around and greet others. You don't know why these other people are in the vet's office. They could be having a disease problem, and you would be exposing your puppy to it. Veterinarians' offices are like human doctors' waiting rooms. Everyone is there to see the doctor, but each has his or her own reason. If someone was coughing and sneezing around you at the doctor's office, you would probably not sit next to them if it could be avoided. Do the same at the veterinarian's office. Do not expose your puppy to more than is absolutely necessary.

The New Home Howl

Oh boy, you have a new puppy! He is so cute and cuddly. It is really fun to watch him play and run around trying to do things that he is not big enough to do yet. You have spent the day with the puppy, making him understand that he is safe and that someone is there to play with him, just like when he was in his litter. You have taken all the precautions to prevent any injury, and helped him stay out of trouble.

Does this sound familiar? You bet it does. Each of us who has ever gotten a puppy has done the same thing. Now it is time for bed. You will go through the same routine that you have been doing before the puppy came. The only problem is that the puppy does not know this sleep-time ritual. He is new to the family (pack), and he does not understand the new rules. He wants you to stay and play with him and make him feel safe. After all, you allowed him to tire and sleep throughout the day, and now he wants to play. You, on the other hand, are ready for bed, and don't want to play. He is placed in his room or crate and told *good night*. The lights are turned out, and everyone goes to bed. Well, at least for about two hours. Then the howling starts.

You get up and reassure the puppy that everything is okay. You go back to bed for about twenty minutes, and the howling starts again. You get up, give him a toy to play with, and go back to bed. About thirty minutes later, he howls—well, you get the picture. After about the fourth time of getting out of bed, you decide that he can howl if he wants, because you are not getting up. One hour later, you are talking to an eight-week-old puppy like it was a human. "What's wrong? You have your toy! I made you a comfortable bed. Please, let me sleep!"

That wonderful little ball of fluff that you placed in the crate has now turned into an ugly monster that will not let you sleep, and you have to go to work in the morning. The howling continues, and you finally give in. You have to get some sleep. So, you get the puppy, place him in bed, and everyone gets some sleep. Great! Except that you have just taught your puppy that he can win through persistence. You have also taught him that he does not have to spend his nights alone. He can join the pack leaders in their bed. <u>Score: Puppy 1, Owners 0.</u>

Your crate should be placed in a room that is farthest away from your bedroom. Place the puppy inside the crate and turn off the lights. The crate will keep him from roaming around, scratching and chewing on everything in sight. Oh yes, new smells and new things must be tasted and chewed. When you place the pup in his crate, you should place a hot water bottle wrapped in a towel inside the crate with him, along with <u>one</u> toy. This will give the pup the feeling of having one of his warm littermates with him, and he will have something to occupy him if he awakens. Remember, this puppy had a lot of company (littermates) around before you came along. Use a sheet or some type of material to cover all sides of the crate, except the door.

At some time during the night, the water bottle is going to cool. The puppy will get uncomfortable and lonely, and he will howl. Let him. If you decide to re-warm the bottle, do not play with or talk to the puppy. Just do what you have to do, re-cover the crate, and go to bed. If you repeatedly get up to reassure the puppy, he is winning the battle, and teaching you to respond to his call. He is calling you to get your attention, and you are responding. Who is training whom? If you do not talk to him, and just do what is necessary, he will learn that bedtime means sleep time. He will fall into the routine in about two days. After two days, you can remove the water bottle. Just be patient and persistent.

If, during the day, the puppy should fall asleep playing, pick him up and place him in his crate with the door open. This will help to train him as to where his sleeping quarters are located. It will also help eliminate that late-night call of being lonely.

HINT: You should take an old face cloth or hand towel with you when you go to pick up your puppy. Have the litter owner rub the female all over her body with the cloth. This will transfer the smells of the mother onto the cloth. Place the cloth in a resealable bag and take it home with you. When placing your puppy in his box or crate, remove the cloth from the bag and place the cloth in with him.

He will now have the smells of Mom, his original owner, and you. This may give the puppy some comfort in his new environment and reduce the howling. When your remove the pup from his crate, remove the cloth and place it in the resealable bag. This will hold the scent on the cloth. Place it in with him again when it is time for sleep. The pup will begin to adjust to the smells of his new home, and the cloth can be disposed of within a few days.

Collar and Leash

Question: When should I place a collar on my puppy?
Answer: Place a collar on your puppy as soon as possible.

You should give the puppy about one week to start making adjustments to his new home. There are new smells, new people, different sounds, completely different surroundings, and the rules have changed from what they were a week ago. This time will give your puppy a chance to adapt to the new things around him. You don't want to make too many changes in his life at one time. A flat-type nylon, cotton, or leather collar should be placed on the puppy. <u>DO NOT</u> use a chain or pinch type collar on a puppy that is less than four months of age. The flat collar should be loose enough that it does not restrict his breathing while running, and tight enough that it will not slip over his head.

A number of people have handled the collar you have purchased, and it has picked up some of the smells of the store from where it was purchased. Before placing the collar on your puppy, rub it in your hands, let him smell it, and then rub it all over him. This will transfer your scent and his scent onto the collar. When the collar is placed on the puppy, give him a few minutes to adjust. He will probably start scratching at it, concerned about something around his neck that was not there before. After he has worn the collar for three to five minutes, take him outside. Once outside, the puppy will forget about the collar, begin playing, and relieve himself. Let him play for fifteen to twenty minutes; then you may bring him back into the house. He probably will have forgotten all about the collar, but he may be reminded when he scratches his neck. If the puppy seems intent on getting the collar off his neck, distract him by playing with him or giving him a toy. After a day of wearing the collar, he will forget he has it on.

I recommend placing the lead (leash) on the puppy only after he has accepted and is used to wearing the collar. Put the lead on him while he is in the house, where he can be supervised. Just as with the collar, the leash will have various smells on it that are unfamiliar to the puppy. Before placing it on the collar, rub the leash in your hands, and let the puppy sniff the leash. Let him investigate all the new smells, but do not let him chew on it. While he is investigating the leash, you should try rubbing the leash on him. Do this slowly so that you do not frighten him or give him cause for concern. This will help to put some of the puppy's scent on the leash and make it more acceptable to him. Once the puppy stops showing interest in the leash, you may attach it to his collar. This process should take about fifteen minutes.

Once the leash is placed on the collar, let the puppy drag the leash around. He will try backing away from it, biting at it, pushing it away with his paws, or running from it. Having this thing trailing around behind him may make him nervous at first, but reassurance and play will help him to ignore it. You must supervise the puppy during this time. If the puppy gets the leash caught on something, release it as fast as possible. You do not want the puppy to be afraid of the leash, so don't let the leash be the cause of any fear or concern for him.

When the puppy has adjusted to the leash, you should pick up the "thumb loop" end and allow the puppy to walk around with you attached. Once he feels confident that there is not any danger, you may begin working with him. If the puppy wants to fight the leash, let him fight. Do not try to force him to come to you or drag him around. No yelling! No jerking the puppy around because he does not do what you want. He does not understand the loss of control and is unsure of it. Just give him time to figure out that he is not going to get away, and that he is safe with this thing on him. He will stop fighting the leash and come to you. Praise him for coming, and let him rest. This will go on for a short time, but the puppy will come to accept the leash.

If your puppy has the confidence to ignore the leash and begins pulling you along to get to where he wants to be, you should follow him and give him time to become accustomed to having the leash on him. After he has adjusted to the lead, about one week, if he still wants to pull you, follow the instructions listed under the chapter on controlled walk. There are other methods, but I like the controlled walk the best.

Chapter 9
Socializing

Socialization has its earliest beginnings while the puppy is still in its litter. Siblings will play and choose the alpha position, while the whelping female monitors the activities. She will allow the puppies to wrestle, fight, and play. Often the rough play will erupt into a skirmish between two siblings, regardless of their sex. The skirmish will end almost as fast as it starts, with the two puppies separating and moving away from each other. This is all part of the social program, pecking order, established by Mother Nature.

By spending time playing and handling the puppies on a daily basis, the breeder is helping the puppies become accustomed to human contact. Play times, human contact, and establishing a pecking order are all important. Each of these actions aids the puppies in learning what is considered acceptable behavior, both in the pack and with humans. Proper handling of the puppies by the breeder, such as petting, touching, playing, and monitoring the behaviors within the litter, is the basis of socialization.

Most behavior problems begin when a puppy is separated from the litter and sent to live with its new owner. If the pup was not adequately handled and socialized by the breeder, then the new owner will begin experiencing some difficulty in handling his dog. This can be seen when the dog cowers or moves away from the touch of the new owner or someone unfamiliar to it, or makes an aggressive action of growling or resisting being handled. These actions, if allowed to continue, could develop into a serious behavior problem, without the new owner ever being aware of it.

The new owner also has an obligation to play with the puppy, in addition to handling it and teaching it what is acceptable behavior within its new pack. When the puppy leaves its litter to be placed with a new owner, the puppy will feel some anxiety when it realizes that it no longer has its littermates or familiar surroundings. This separation can be identified when the puppy is left alone on its first night in its new home, and you hear the new home howl. He is lonely, but he must learn that he now sleeps alone. This is the first lesson in proper behavior and socialization in his new home.

Your new puppy will require and should receive a lot of attention. Introducing your puppy to guests and your other pets will help with the socialization process. This will help the puppy develop confidence, but you must be cautious. The introductions should be performed in a controlled environment, so as not to create a fearful situation or cause any harm to come to him. Exposing your puppy to all of these different smells, sounds, animals, and people will help him to relax and accept these things as normal. Once he is accustomed to these things, he will readily pay more attention to you. He may be momentarily distracted by a sound or person, but he will come to understand that you are always there and in charge, even though everything else is different.

When being introduced to someone or something new, your dog may react in a surprised, fearful, or hesitant manner. The reason for this is that each of us has a different scent or smell about us. It is one of the things that make us unique and easily identifiable to the dog. It is better to allow the puppy to make the initial contact with a person, rather than submit him to rapid changes by passing him from one person to another. Instead of passing him from person to person, place him on the floor and allow him to investigate the new visitor at his own pace. As he warms up to the new person, they may pet and reassure him.

Notice how a dog will sniff and investigate a new toy or gift that you provide. Keep in mind that a number of people touched that item long before you purchased it. Those smells are still there, and he wants to be sure that it is safe before he touches it.

Think of scent as a vial of ammonia. When you open a bottle of ammonia, you can identify the strong odor from a short distance, and without any discomfort. However, if you place the bottle close to your nose and smell it, you will withdraw your head from it and feel a burning sensation deep in your nose. This is the same reaction your dog is having to the smell of other humans. His sense of smell is much greater than yours, and thrusting him toward someone unfamiliar to him is similar to placing your nose in a vial of ammonia. Let the puppy make the first contact, and he will adjust.

Once the puppy has had all of its shots, and you are ready to expose your puppy to the world, take it slowly, allowing him time to adjust to the sounds and smells of the various areas you visit. Some of the best places to take your puppy are playgrounds and parks. You just cannot take a puppy to a playground or park without someone wanting to pet it.

Other places that aid in the socialization are pet stores, home-improvement centers, large department outlets, small shopping centers, and mini-malls. Here you will not only come into contact with people, but experience a large variety of sounds, horns blowing, cars moving about, doors opening and closing, merchandise being moved about, a variety of different odors, and a hustle and bustle of people in motion. People never really listen to the sounds in or near a shopping center. If you were to take the time to just walk around and listen, you would be amazed at all the things you hear. Just take some time to listen. No talking, just listening. Once you do this, you will understand why this is such a good area to work with your dog.

You do not have to enter these facilities; just walk your dog in the parking lot or on the sidewalk if one is available. If you are not sure whether your dog will be welcomed, just ask the manager for permission and explain to him what you are doing. Most pet stores do not mind having your dog walk around inside the store as long as it is on a lead and under control. This is also a good time to practice your obedience commands.

Keep in mind that all of this is new to him, and he will want to be cautious. Do not force him into a situation or be overly protective. Both of these actions can cause problems later on in his life. Once he has adjusted to the area, you may begin working with him. You must be in control of the dog in order to protect him and those meeting him. All you have to do is walk your puppy or stand outside of the door and wait for people to walk by. As they do, ask them to pet your dog. Keep in mind that not all people will be willing to pet a strange dog, so do not be offended by those who say no. Dog lovers are in the minority, and you must respect the desires of those who are not fond of dogs and are not comfortable around them. This includes puppies. Those who do pet your dog should be informed to pet him without patting him on the head or making any sudden movements toward him. Patting a dog on top of his head will disrupt his ability to focus. Repeatedly patting him on the head may make him hand shy, and he will try to avoid your touch. Sudden movements could startle him, and that could create other problems in the future. You want to reassure the dog that meeting new people is a good experience. With other animals, be sure that they are also on a lead and can be controlled. You do not want your dog to be traumatized by another animal, so proceed with caution

The idea behind a group training class is to teach the dog to obey the owner in basic obedience commands and movements, and to receive socialization from the other dogs and people in the class. My recommendation is that even if you are attending a formal obedience class, you should take your dog to other locations, such as parks, shopping center parking lots, etc., to aid him in being a social animal. There is no such thing as too much socialization. The more a dog is socialized, the easier it is to handle him, and fewer behavior problems will be encountered. A well-socialized dog will make your life much easier, and his life much simpler.

Since you are going to be in public locations with your dog, do not forget to bring some plastic bags with you so you can clean up the area when your dog relieves himself. You are responsible for your dog and his actions, so be a responsible owner. Clean up after your dog. After all, you would not want to step in that stuff if you were out shopping.

Chapter 10
Equipment

Collars

Before you can begin training your dog, you should understand the use of some of the training equipment that is available to you, and its purpose. Let us start with the types of collars.

FLAT COLLARS

The flat collar is the type of collar that your dog should wear all the time. It may be made of leather, cotton, nylon, or a combination of nylon fiber and plastic. It may have a buckle or a snap-latch-type closure, and a D-ring. The D-ring is where you will attach your lead. This is the type of collar your dog should wear daily, and the one where the registration, identification, and/or rabies vaccination tag should be attached.

Buckle-type collars will have pre-punched holes approximately one inch apart. Measure your dog's neck, and add two inches to the measurement. The sum of the two is the collar size your dog will need. This will provide enough room for comfort, control, and some growth. You simply place it on the dog's neck and tighten the collar strap to the hole that will give a comfortable fit without being able to slide over the dog's head when buckled. To adjust the collar, move the strap either upward or downward until the collar fits properly. If your dog's neck is an odd size, you may punch another hole between the pre-punched holes to help it fit   properly.

The snap-type collars are arranged as one strap that is turned on itself with an adjusting tab to gain the proper fit. Instead of a buckle, it has two interlocking pieces that will snap together to ensure closure. These collars are produced in three or four adjustable sizes, depending on the manufacturer, with adjustments varying from four to ten inches. Measure your dog's neck and choose the collar size accordingly. The collar is arranged so that adjustments may be made while your dog is wearing it. To adjust the fit of this collar, you simply slide the adjusting tab upward or downward until the proper fit is obtained.

Snap-type latches are made of hard plastic, and hold up surprisingly well. Although it is durable and easily adjustable, I have found that the buckle can be broken. Large dogs that pull strongly in situations where they are determined to get at something may cause enough pressure for the snap to break, leaving you in an awkward position. I like the convenience of the snap-type latch collars and use them when the dogs are in their kennels or not working on a lead.

Leather collars are equipped with a buckle, D-ring, and pre-punched holes. Leather collars will dry out and crack if proper care and maintenance are not given to them. There are cleaning agents and oil treatments that can be used to keep them looking nice and prevent them from drying out. If maintained properly, the leather collars will give years of use.

Cotton collars may have a buckle or a snap-type latch. They may be washed by hand or placed in a washing machine. Keep in mind that cotton will shrink to some degree, so when you place the collar on the dog, you must ensure a proper fit. With the buckle-type collar, you may have to punch a new hole in it, because the weave is such that the buckle pin will not fit into the weave without making a hole.

Nylon collars may have a buckle or snap-type latch. They may also be washed by hand or in a washing machine. The buckle type will need to be adjusted the same as the cotton one after washing. The difference between other materials and the nylon-type collar is that this material needs to be bonded when it is cut. If it is not bonded, it will fray, and heat is the best way to do this. When making another hole in this collar, it is advisable to use a heated metal punch that will penetrate the material and leave it bonded as it passes through it. Care should be taken when punching nylon. The heat tends to turn the material into a plastic-type substance. If touched prior to cooling, it will stick to your skin and cause a burn.

PROPER PLACEMENT: The flat collar should be placed around your dog's neck with enough room for a comfortable fit.

Purchase a collar that will fit your dog's neck size, and not one that is oversized. Purchasing the larger collar with the idea that he will grow into it will cause improper fit, discomfort, and enable the dog to slip out of the collar. Having the ability to slip out of the collar reduces your ability to control the dog and increases the chances of serious injury to your dog. As your dog grows, it is better to replace the collar with one that fits properly.

Puppy — The collar should fit around the neck so it cannot be pulled over its head. Check the collar often, as your puppy is growig, because he will soon outgrow the fit.

Adult or large dog — The collar should be snug enough so that you can place two fingers under the collar, or approximately one inch of free space. When making the two-finger measurement, do so as if you were measuring liquid in a glass. Place your forefinger and second finger together. Place both fingers under the collar with your forefinger resting against the dog's neck. There should be enough room between the collar and the dog's neck for your fingers to fit snugly but comfortably. If it is too loose, the dog will be able to slip his head out of the collar, and perhaps cause you anxiety over his being freed from your control.

CHAIN COLLARS

Chain collars, often referred to as choke chains, are metal collars that look like automobile tow chains, but in much smaller dimensions. Chain collars come in various sizes, shapes, and thicknesses. The collar must be two to three inches larger than the measurement of your dog's neck. If it is less than two or more than three inches larger, you will not be able to achieve the proper timing required for a correction. Chain collars are made in even sizes. If your dog's neck measures an even size, you will need a collar two inches larger. If your dog's neck is an odd size, you will need the collar three inches larger.

The chain collars also come in different shapes. The most common one is the medium-linked chain. The others are the larger-linked "fur-saving" collar and the smaller-linked show chain or slip collar.

The larger-linked "fur-saving" collars are meant for use on dogs with long hair. The makers of these collars profess that they will not tangle or pull the hair. I find these types harder to use and release, even when the proper size is worn. The larger links do not move as fluidly as the medium- or smaller-linked chains, and it takes some time and practice for the handler to become accustomed to them.

The show chain or slip collar is used when your dog is in the show ring. I do not recommend using this collar in training. This collar is meant for minor corrections and to remind the dog that you are in control. It is not meant for training, and it could cause injury to a dog that is not trained, or it could break, leaving you in an awkward position without any control. The prevention of injury and the dog's safety should be the most important consideration in any type of training.

The varying thicknesses of all chain collars are to compensate for the weight of your dog and the amount of pull that can be applied. Each chain is rated by the weight of your dog. If your dog's weight is at the top end of the recommendation, then purchase the next recommended level.

A chain collar is commonly referred to as a "choke chain." I prefer calling these type of collars "correction collars." The difference is in the manner of placement around the dog's neck. If improperly placed on the dog, it will not release when the lead is slackened. The collar will remain tight around the dog's neck and pose a choking threat, or it will only release due to the muscular structure of the dog's neck. If it is placed on the dog properly, it will release when slack is placed in the lead, will not pose any threat, and will make the dog more responsive.

PROPER PLACEMENT: There are two circular rings on the chain collar. There is a ring attached to each end of the chain. Hold the collar with a ring in each hand. Pass the chain through one of the rings. Place your hand in the chain and hold it up in front of you so that the chain now forms the letter "P." Place the chain over your right hand as if you were going to wear the chain on your wrist. Now, <u>facing your dog</u>, hold him with your left hand. Grab his muzzle with your right hand, and using your left hand, slide the chain off your arm and over his head. It may be a little snug going over his head, but it must fit properly around his neck. If the collar is too tight going over the dog's head, then it is advisable to move up to the next size collar.

NOTE:

1. When removing this collar, do so by pulling the chain over one ear at a time. Pulling it over both ears at the same time may pinch his ears and cause him to fear the chain.

2. This collar should never be allowed to remain on an unsupervised dog. If it were to get caught on anything, it would cause a choking sensation. The dog, in an attempt to free itself from this threat, could end up choking himself to death.

PINCH OR PRONG COLLARS

The pinch collar is commonly referred to as the prong collar because of the inverted prong arrangement of the collar. This collar is made with links of inverted steel prongs circling the dog's neck and a chain configuration attaching the ends together. The chain attachment will have a large circular ring where the lead will be attached to the collar. No adjustments are made to the chain portion of the collar. The collar is placed on the dog by separating one of the links and placing it around the dog's neck in the same manner as a flat collar. Adjustments are made by adding or removing the pronged links. The end links should never be removed, as they are the key to this collar.

Although this collar has a medieval look, it does not puncture or poke the dog's neck. It is designed to gather up the skin around the dog's neck and create a pinching action, as opposed to a choking action. The pinch collar has been used very effectively by slight-of-build persons who have a very large or hard-pulling dog. It gives them the added advantage they need to control the dog.

It should be noted that this collar is not recommended for use on very submissive or aggressive dogs. If placed on a submissive dog, it may create a greater problem of submissiveness, or the dog may strike out in fear. If placed on an aggressive dog, it will serve as an agitation device, and the dog may become more aggressive. The pinch collar is a very useful tool that has been slighted by those who do not understand its use and who view it as an abusive device.

PROPER PLACEMENT: The collar should be fitted snugly around the dog's neck, but not pushing into the skin. The chain portion must be fully extended as a part of the collar, and there should be enough room for the collar to slide around the dog's neck. With this configuration, it will require only a minimum of strength to apply a proper correction. Do not make forceful corrections with this collar, as they may cause undue pain and instill fear in your dog.

HEAD COLLARS

These collars are placed around the dog's head and muzzle. It serves to keep the dog's head pointed toward you. This is an exceptional tool when working with a dog that tends to fight or not pay attention to you. Using this type of collar can help an aggressive dog learn to tolerate the presence of unknown people and dogs. The lead is attached to a D-ring located on the collar under the dog's lower jaw.

Since you control the dog's head with this collar, you are able to turn your dog away from what is causing his inappropriate action, and guide him into acceptance of the situation. This type of collar does not create any undue stress or confusion, which could be created with a chain- or pinch-type collar. Learning the proper use of this collar is very important. Timing and exposure are the keys to being successful with this collar, and it can be very effective.

ELECTRONIC COLLARS

The electronic collar, or shock collar, can be an excellent tool when training a stubborn dog, a dog that is out of your reach, or a dog that has become "leash wise." The phrase "leash wise" refers to the dog that will work well while it is on a leash but refuses to obey when it is off. This collar is very effective in breaking bad habits, such as biting, growling, running away, car chasing, and refusing to come from a distance. It has been used effectively on working dogs by helping them understand the command from the handler at a distance. It can be used to teach enthusiastic working dogs by preventing them from being hurt by animals much larger than they are. Most dogs can be taught to obey without the use of an electronic collar, and this equipment should be used sparingly, or when all other methods have failed to produce results. These collars are meant for use on adult dogs and should never be used on a puppy. Timing is extremely important when using this collar. A correction given at the wrong time, or inappropriately, may cause the dog to react to something other than your intention. Caution must be observed with this equipment.

The collar, or receiver, is arranged with a battery and two electrodes on a flat collar. The collar is placed snugly around the dog's neck, with the electrodes touching firmly against the dog so that the collar does not move around. Be careful not to place the collar too tightly around the dog's neck, otherwise, breathing will be very difficult.

The transmitter is arranged with varying levels of intensity, which are selected by the handler. When the buttons are pressed, they trigger the receiver, and the dog receives a shock. The shock lasts only as long as you hold down the button.

The greatest error made with this collar is to set the sensor level on the highest setting and continue to use it at this level. Manufacturers recommend you start with the lowest setting and work upward until you see a response from the dog. I find this contradictory to effective training. I find it better to evaluate the attitude of the dog to determine what level will suffice. Your objective is to get his attention and halt the action. As with any correction method, the first correction should be the harshest, and the next correction should be a reminder. First, get a positive response from the dog, and then go to a lower setting. The response will be such that the dog's attention will be taken away from the improper action. When the undesired action is stopped, give a command that the dog understands and praise the dog for the desired action. If the dog should return to the action, then a lower setting should be used to tingle the dog to remind him of the error. Using this method, I find that I only have to use the electronic collar two to three times. If the dog should forget itself in the next training session, the lower setting will remind him of the correction, and he will give the desired action.

The electronic collar is an expensive piece of equipment which, when used properly, can achieve rapid results; however, if used improperly, it can ruin a good dog. I recommend that a long line, approximately twenty-five to thirty feet long, be used when training for the first time with the electronic collar. If the dog should become excited and run away, you will have a means of stopping him.

I know of a trainer who placed one of these collars on a dog that had a car-chasing problem. The trainer did not use a long line with the collar. As a truck pulled onto their property, the dog began to bark. As the truck began to leave, the dog ran toward the truck and began barking again. A verbal command to stop was given, and a signal sent. The dog did not stop. Immediately, the setting was pushed to the limit. Another verbal command and signal was sent. The dog jumped up into the air as if it were an acrobat, turned completely around, and landed on all four feet. It turned around again and never stopped running. The dog and a very expensive collar were never seen again.

Had the dog been worked on a long line prior to the electronic collar, or in conjunction with an electronic collar, it would have had an idea of what the trainer wanted it to do. If the long line had been used in conjunction with the electronic collar, the dog could have been guided back to the trainer, demonstrating the desired action, and would not have been able to run away.

LEADS AND LEASHES

The tool used to attach a dog to its handler is known as a leash or lead. Leads come in a variety of styles, lengths, and widths, but all serve the same function: They prevent the dog from leaving its handler and provide a means of keeping the dog under control.

Leads may be made of leather, nylon, cotton, or chain. There is a loop handle on one end and a snap on the other. There are varying lengths, from two to forty feet, to accommodate training, showing, or working the dog. The two-foot lead is used for showing large dogs or limiting their range of movement. The four- and six-foot leads are the ones most commonly used for training and/or showing.

Long lines are lengths of light line or leash material that are fashioned in the shape of a lead, and give you the ability to gain distance from the dog while maintaining a degree of control. These lines may be purchased in lengths of ten, twenty, twenty-five, thirty, and forty feet. Long lines may be made by purchasing a length of "pull cord" from your local hardware store. The size pull cord needed is the type used for starting chainsaws and grass-trimmers. Next, attach a bull snap similar to the type used on a lead, to one end, and you're ready to begin. This line will be light enough that the dog will ignore it, but strong enough to stop him.

The loop handle should be placed on the thumb, with the lead wrapped around the hand one time in a downward fashion, and have the remainder of the lead leaving the bottom of the hand. Example: Hold out your right hand as if you were going to shake hands with someone. Place the loop on your thumb, and wrap the lead around your hand once, moving in a downward direction first. With the lead wrapped in this manner, should an accident occur, all you have to do is open your hand to allow a release of the lead. If the handle was placed around the wrist and you were to fall, the lead would not come off of your hand so easily. The dog would be able to pull on you, or, if you have a large dog, it could drag you along the ground.

With your left hand, grasp the lead portion closest to the dog. Gather up the remaining lead in your right hand, or allow it to hang loosely in front of you. This method will give you greater leverage when making a correction, and it will provide a means of a quick release, if necessary. The lead should not be pulled tightly, creating pressure on the dog's neck. It should hang from the dog's collar so that there is approximately three to four inches of slack. With this slack, you may make whatever corrections are necessary, and the dog will not feel any pressure on his neck. Too much pressure on the dog's neck will cause him to rebel and fight the lead. Given enough slack so as not to create any stress or threat to the dog will have him walking beside you without any trouble. This will be covered again in the training sections.

When purchasing a lead, be sure to get one that will be comfortable for you and your dog. If the lead is too wide, or the snap too heavy, it will be cumbersome, preventing proper corrections, and creating problems for the dog. What you are looking for is a lead that will hang down from the collar when released, will be easy to operate, and be strong enough to hold the pulling dog. I find starting with a one-half-inch or five-eighths-inch cotton lead that is six feet long, and a twenty-foot length of long line to be adequate for most training. The choice of material is a matter of taste. Choose the one that you like and are comfortable using. This will help you to achieve the desired results.

Training Tabs are very short sections of material, made from nylon line or leather, and are approximately two to three inches in length, with a bull snap attached to one end. This tab is used when introducing a dog to "off-lead" training. The tab would attach to the D-ring on the collar, and under the dog's neck. Instead of using a lead for your corrections, you would use the tab.

Chapter 11
Attitude and Posture

Prior to engaging in any type of training, you must understand the influence and effect that your attitude and body posture will have on your dog. Knowing how to stand and keeping calm will help you get farther, faster with your training sessions.

Owners cause the majority of the problems seen in dogs. Yes, owners who have become so anxious about training that they lose control or attempt to apply human logic to their training. Dogs do not learn through logic. They learn through repetitive actions and their basic canine instincts. In order for you to achieve the desired results, you will have to think like a dog. I know that this sounds strange, but it is true. If you continually apply human logic to your training sessions, your dog may become confused by the mixed signals, commands, and body language.

Posturing, or body language, is one of the means of communication among canines. Have you ever watched two dogs when they first meet? They will become very stiff and move about slowly, sniffing each other and gathering identifying information. This posturing allows the dogs to set the tempo for the meeting. If there is a disagreement between them, one will utter a low growl, then rise up on his toes to make himself taller than the other. This action causes a reaction from the other dog that will raise the hair on his back to make him appear larger and taller than the first. At this point is where most dogfights will begin. If you watch carefully, you will notice that all fights begin in the air, and not on the ground. They will clash together with each standing tall on their hind legs, and from there, the fight will go to the ground.

Due to his heightened awareness of body posture, your dog can determine your mood without your having to say a word. He can make the determination that you are not in a good mood, and will generally try to console you. Of course, most humans misread the signals and take this as an aggravating action by the dog. You cannot make them believe everything is all right when it is not. When they can read your body language and know your mood and attitude, it is difficult to fool them.

The tone of your voice will also enable your dog to determine your present attitude. If your voice is soft and gentle, or sweet-sounding, the dog will respond to you more readily. If you are loud, gruff, or boisterous, your dog will approach with caution. Owners sometimes read this as the dog being submissive. Well, if you talked to me in those gruff tones, I too would be a little reserved about approaching you!

Look at how a trainer goes about dealing with a new dog. He never approaches a dog in a manner that could be perceived by the dog as a threat. He is not dealing with logic; he is dealing with animal instincts. Approach the dog in a soft and caring manner, as you would like to be approached. Talking in soft and soothing tones will relax the dog, and he will not feel threatened. Once this is accomplished, training may begin slowly. Only minor corrections should be made, in order to avoid being misread by the dog. If a correction is in order, it is made swiftly and sharply. It should not be made to the level of causing anxiety in the dog, but enough to get his attention. This procedure is used to make the dog understand that the handler is in charge and must be obeyed, but he is not causing the dog any anxiety or giving it cause for fear. He is making the dog understand that he must be respected.

When approaching a dog for training, do not grovel. Walk to him standing tall. You are considered the alpha figure, and bending down and groveling for the dog will only have him challenge you for authority in the future. When you bend down to the dog, you are lowering yourself to his level. Putting yourself on his level will sometimes have him challenge you for leadership. Let him know in the beginning that you are in charge and your authority must be obeyed, but not to the level of causing the dog to fear you.

When a dog has done something that upsets an otherwise normal routine, most people will begin yelling at the dog and questioning it about its actions. The dog has no idea about what is going on, only that you are upset. I have had people say repeatedly that the dog knows he did wrong because of the way he responds when questioned by them. He is not aware of any wrongdoing. He is aware that you are upset by your tone of voice and body language. What occurs in most of these cases is that the dog has become conditioned to the attitude and body language you are displaying. It has been written that asking a dog "What have you done?" causes the dog to slink away from the owner. The owner says, "He knows he did something wrong; that's why he acts that way." This is incorrect. Your body posture and the tone of your voice are keys to the dog's knowing that you are upset, not what he has done wrong.

To prove this, I have taken dogs that were asked a specific question, then substituted other words, but used the same tone and body language, only to have the dogs slink away. If the sound and action are similar, the dog will react … period. Let us say that you are upset and ask the dog a question, as if he's going to tell you the answer. You come into a room, drop whatever it is you are holding, and say, "What did you do?" The reaction you get from the dog is that he hangs his head and tries to slink away, but you call him and he slithers toward you.

Maintaining that same attitude, voice tone, and body posture, perform the same routine but substitute this phrase. "What if I love you?" The phrase sounds silly, I know, but it is similar in sound to the other question. The dog hears the beginning "What," and it is enough for him. You are in a bad mood, and the best place he can be is far away from you while you develop a better attitude. You assume this to be the dog knowing he has done something wrong. He only knows that your attitude and body language say you are going to cause him some form of punishment, and he really does not know why.

If he has done something wrong, and you did not see it happen within three seconds of the incident, the dog probably has forgotten the entire situation. Correcting him ten seconds after it has occurred is too late, so coming home hours after the incident and making a correction will only serve to confuse the dog. He will begin reacting to your arrival as the time for his punishment.

Your dog can read you within the first three seconds of greeting you. He knows from the manner you carry yourself and the sound of your voice the kind of day you are having. Take the time to understand that dogs do not think like humans. You see someone carrying on because they are upset, and you want to stand clear of them. Your dog just wants to console you and make you feel better. Do not let your bad day turn into a bad session with your dog. By the way, dogs do *not* spend their day trying to find ways to upset you.

Stand tall and talk in soothing tones. You will get more out of your dog ... and most people.

Chapter 12
Discipline

T he word *discipline* seems to strike terror in the hearts of some owners. I do not know how this word came to be interpreted as a brutal beating, but beating your dog is not the form of training that you should ever need to use. There are techniques that will place you in charge of your dog. He will come to understand that you are in control and that you must be obeyed.

What is discipline? Discipline is defined as "activity, exercise, or a regimen that develops or improves a skill." This sounds simple enough, and it actually is very simple.

How can discipline make anyone eager to learn? Your dog wants to please you, and he will, if he knows and understands the rules. If you do not apply or enforce any rules, the dog will behave in the same manner prescribed for survival within the pack. He will assume the position of leader and attempt to make you follow his rules. In other words, the dog will train you. Dogs like knowing the rules. Like their human counterpart, knowing the rules results in being able to continue in a lifestyle without any repercussions. Having control of your dog will make it much easier to teach him, and he will be eager to learn.

In the pack, there is a leader, the alpha dog. The leader sets the rules, and the rest follow those rules. If they do not, the leader disciplines them without fail. There is not a "second chance" at proper behavior within the pack.

The first step of enforcement could be a low growl. This is the same warning you give when you say "Ah, ah" or "Don't do that." If the warning is not effective, a physical one is applied. The correction comes rapidly, and it is over in an instant. It would appear as if the leader had just torn a piece of flesh from the violator. Upon closer examination, the violator will only have some saliva on its coat with no broken skin.

Generally, a vicious fight will only occur under the following conditions: 1) when there is a challenge for the leadership (alpha) position; 2) in defense of territory or possessions; 3) to be the first to breed any females. The third will cause more dogfights than any other reason.

If you have never seen the discipline inflicted by a pack leader on its followers, you should view some of the films that have been produced on this subject. These include, but are not limited to, *The Wolf Pack* and *The Wild Dog Pack*. The educational channels and some National Wildlife programming will show these periodically. You may contact the television stations in your area for information on how to acquire some of the videotapes, or you may make inquiries of your local Wildlife & Fisheries Department.

Both of the actions, the growl and the actual physical contact, are forms of discipline. The difference between the two is that one is vocal and the other is physical. Both have a purpose, and each should be administered as needed.

There has been much debate over the use—or misuse—of the words *correction* and *discipline.*

Correction — Punishment intended to improve.

Discipline — Controlled behavior resulting from training.

Without corrections to improve desired behavior, you cannot achieve discipline. As you read on, you will see both words used. You must understand that you will first teach the dog whatever action you want it to perform. Corrections are made after the dog understands the action but refuses to comply. By doing this, you will achieve discipline. Do not let the words confuse you.

A female with her litter of puppies displays another good example of correction and discipline. Puppies are always in need of something, whether it is food, affection, play, comfort, or attention. If you observe the female with her litter, you will see her nudge the pups with her nose to move them. If a puppy decides to ignore the nudges and persist in the undesired action, the female will growl at the pup. If he continues, she strikes out fast, hard, and with conviction. The pup will then run to the far side of the house/kennel, squealing as if he had just lost a body part. The female will ignore his whimpering and go on about her business. On the pup's next approach, she will lick him and pay more attention to him.

This is the method used by the female to teach discipline. She corrects the pup for not obeying the command to stop. She does it the instant she is not obeyed, and makes the correction one to remember. Then, after the incident is over and the pup has time to let the lesson sink in, she goes back to being "Mom" and gives him the same attention that the others in the litter would receive. What you learn from this is that patience, timing, and consistency are important rules in training. 1) The correction must be at the right time. 2) You must be consistent if you are to achieve the desired results. 3) You must display some patience when training.

Leash corrections are performed differently than those made by electronic methods. With a leash, the dog understands that you are the one making the correction. With an e-collar, they have no idea where the correction originated.

A correction should be applied only after the dog is taught to understand what is expected of him. You will use varying forms of corrections, none of which should exceed the level of attaining a *yelp*.

115

This is the highest level of discipline that will ever be enforced. Each dog has its own sensitivity level, and you must realize the degree of strength and timing required to achieve the proper correction. Start by making a mild correction and increase the intensity until you achieve a response. Most dogs will respond without having to administer a harsh correction. If a dog is disciplined too harshly, or if it is disciplined continuously without understanding what is expected, it will generally cower, roll over on its back submissively, urinate, defecate, try to escape your presence by struggling with the lead, or bite at the handler.

If any of these things occur while you are training your dog, stop training. Put everything away for that day and start fresh the next day. Keep in mind that you went too far previously, and work accordingly.

Your goal is to have a dog that performs to please its master, and not one that responds out of fear or cowers at your every move. You do not want to break the dog's spirit. You just want him to learn the rules and obey them.

Now that you understand the highest level of correction to be applied, let me explain how the lead and collar work together. When a correction is made, it is done with the lead attached to the collar. You will pull the lead sharply in the direction of the required correction. Direction of correction is discussed in each of the chapters on training, such as heel, sit, stay, etc. When the correction is made, it must come swiftly and in a timely manner. Do not wait until the dog has made a mistake and is walking around before you make the correction. It must be made the instant the dog begins to disobey.

Regardless of which discipline you are working on, the correction must be swift. You will pull the lead sharply in the direction required, and release it faster than you made the correction. This takes a little time to understand, so I will give you a method of practicing.

Have someone hold the lead in their fist and place it against their chest. Tell them to hold their hand firmly so that you cannot move it. Pull gently on the lead, and you will see that you have to exert a certain amount of strength to move the whole person, but the hand does not move. You are using strength to overpower, and not technique to make a correction. Now doing the same thing, allow a little slack in the lead between you and the person holding the lead. Instead of pulling it, snap the lead quickly and with enough force to move the hand about two inches away from their body, and release the pull so that their hand goes back to their chest. When you can achieve this action, you are now ready to attempt to make the correction on your dog. You now have the method and must find the amount of pull required to get your dog's attention. Remember, you are not trying to choke him, or cause him pain. You are simply getting his attention.

On the subject of leads, never hit your dog with the lead. It is not necessary, and it confuses the dog. He is expected to walk with the lead, and hitting him with it will only cause him to fear it. I would be a little reluctant to walk with you as well.

Trainers will refer to some dogs as being "soft." This is not to imply that the dog is a sissy or a wimp. It refers to the dog's level of sensitivity. Soft dogs will emit a yelp with a mild correction. I have seen soft dogs in all breeds. They can overcome their shyness and submissiveness, but it requires a lot of work and patience. Harsh corrections on this type of dog will ruin the dog. Any form of physical discipline may create a greater problem than the one you are having with a soft dog, so you must go slowly.

Discipline is not just a matter of strength or being able to jerk a dog around by its neck until it yelps. Discipline requires timing and consistency. Giving a dog a command and repeating it, administering a correction, and waiting for a response without instruction are a waste of your time, and serve only to confuse the dog. Instruct, praise, command, and discipline. These are the actions of a leader. You are the leader, and your dog will now respect you, since you followed the rules of the pack.

Timing is the single most important aspect of administering a correction. Once he has learned a command, the dog should be allowed three seconds in which to respond to your command. If you give your dog a command and he does not respond to that command within three seconds, a correction is in order. The correction should be sharp, immediate, and of the proper level to get his attention. If the dog appears confused by the correction, or he does not respond, do not give him another correction. Instead, show him what you want him to do in the following manner: 1) Repeat the command; 2) Help him to assume the position or action required; 3) Place a slight pressure on the lead in the same direction as you would to administer the correction; 4) Praise him when he does it correctly. Praise for a good job or obeying a command will help to convince your dog that he has pleased you; 5) Repeat the entire process as many times as necessary for the dog to understand the command. Once he understands that he will be praised for obeying a command, you will not have to use that correction as often to get him to respond. He will respond because he knows it pleases you, and he will get a reward of praise for doing so.

The three-second rule holds true for most training. Once a dog is trained to perform and does not respond within three seconds of a command, there are two possible explanations: Either he does not understand what is expected of him or he has decided to test you. If he does not understand the command, you must teach him. If he is testing you, you must show him that you are still in charge by using a correction.

This brings us to a point that will be discussed again: NEVER call your dog to you to discipline him. If you are having trouble with your dog and he needs discipline, go to him. Calling your dog to administer a discipline will make your dog think that your calling him is the first step of a discipline. For example, you walk outside of your home and find that your garden has been dug up. You did not see your dog do it, but you are sure he is the culprit. You call your dog, bring him to the hole, and show him what he has done. You tell him he is bad, you slap him with your hand, and you tell him to go lie down. This scenario repeats itself every day.

Let us break this down, step by step. You see a hole in the garden, a place you have spent hours preparing with pride, and now it is destroyed. In all likelihood, your dog was around while you were turning up the soil. Hey, you were digging, so it must be okay to dig in this spot. Even if he did not see you digging, there are scents of decay that you do not smell and your dog does. Curiosity! Where is that smell coming from?

You call your dog so you can show him the hole. Are you encouraging him to dig again? You ask him if he knows what he did, as if he understands what you are asking. You did not catch him in the act, and you do not know how long it has been since the hole was dug. Disciplining at this time is useless. The dog has no idea of what rule he has violated.

You spank the dog. Wrong! Placing your hands on your dog is a sign of approval, even when you feel that you are disciplining him. You are giving mixed signals here. Instead of understanding what he has done wrong, the dog is confused. You called him, and now you are going to discipline him. He believes he is being disciplined for coming to you when you called. Then, you tell him to go lie down, which is probably what he was doing before you called. After all, digging a hole will tire you out. Remember? All you have accomplished is to tell your dog what a wonderful job he has done. Your dog believes that since you put your hands all over him, you must approve of his actions. Moreover, he will probably do it again, in an attempt to please you.

Unless you catch him in the act, disciplining is useless. He does not understand what is happening. All he really knows is that you called him, he came, and you beat him for coming.

Whenever you call your dog, you must praise him for coming. Make his coming to you the most enjoyable thing he will ever encounter. When your dog thinks he will be rewarded for doing what you tell him, he will perform without hesitation.

So what you have learned here is that discipline will only be achieved if the needed correction is applied at the instant it is required. There are other methods of achieving desired results that have been devised by other trainers, and they will have you believe that administering this type of correction is barbarous. Nevertheless, keep in mind that throughout the thousands of years of the dog's existence, the corrections made by a female within the litter or the alpha figure in a pack have never been modified, simplified, or changed. People devise methods and systems that are contrary to what is natural to the dog. I am not saying that other systems will not work. What I am saying is that the dogs understand this method, primarily, because it is the one they were taught from birth, and the one that is performed instinctually.

Chapter 13
Praise and Rewards

P raise and rewards are a necessary part of training, and must be used sparingly and consistently. Praising your dog for doing what you have asked is a reassurance to the dog, and he will attempt to perform in the same manner so that you will give him that same praise.

What is praise? Praise is telling your dog what a good job he has done and placing your hands on him simultaneously.

Verbal praise is the pleasant sound a dog hears when his handler voices approval for an action to a command.

Physical praise is placing your hands on your dog.

Anytime you place your hands on your dog, you are telling him that you accept the behavior he has shown. Your hands are the loving acceptance that the dog wants to feel. Even if you use those same hands to make a correction by slapping your dog, he will think that you are accepting what he has done. I am not saying that you should slap your dog; I am trying to show you that your hands are very important in training. For example: You come home and find your dog's head deep into the garbage can. You yell at him, grab him by the collar, shove his head back into the garbage and then you slap him a number of times. What have you taught your dog?

Let us look at it from the dog's perspective.

First, you came in and yelled. Your dog thinks, "What a strange bark my owner has." Then you grabbed him by the collar, the same area you grab when you want to play, instruct, or dress your dog. Next, you shoved his head back into the garbage. Your dog thinks, "Well, this is where I wanted to be in the first place." Last, you pull him out and slap, slap, slap the devil out of him. Your dog thinks, "Wow! My master really praises hard. It must be praise, because his hands are all over me. They must like what I have done. I'll do it again." The lesson you have taught your dog is that it is okay for him to dig into the garbage.

There are those who will tell you that if a dog jumps up on you, you should push him away and tell him "bad dog." I have seen it repeatedly. The owner pushes the dog away, and the dog jumps right back on the owner. The owner gets frustrated and wants to beat the dog for not listening to his commands. The problem stems from the fact that his hands are on the dog when he pushes him off. The dog thinks this is a game approved by the owner. The dog perceives the touching as approval and wants to keep playing the game. There are other methods to stop these types of behavior, and they are discussed in later chapters. The point I'm making here is that when you put your hands on your dog, he believes he is being praised.

Whenever your dog has performed in a positive manner, you must praise him by repeating the command and placing your hands on him in approval. For example: You tell your dog, "Sit." He sits; you say, "Good boy, good sit," and then you pet him for approximately two to three seconds. This is all of the praise required. Simply apply a couple of pats from you to express your acceptance. If you give him too much praise, he will be distracted from the lesson, lose focus, think that the lesson is over, and will want to play. The trick is to keep him focused on the lesson, but with just enough praise to make him feel that he has done well, so that he wants to do it again.

When punishment is administered with the use of your hands, your dog will be confused by the change in your body posture, tone of voice, and demeanor. In this state of confused and mixed signals, the dog will assume a cowed position and will be very reluctant to approach you. Your dog will begin to approach you cowed down and almost crawling, if he will approach you at all. When this occurs, the dog has lost trust in its master, and it will take a much greater amount of time to regain that trust. Never use your hands for punishment, and *never* beat your dog.

Rewards are given the same as praise. Giving your pet a treat is okay, but I believe that a dog should learn to accept petting or praise more than treats. After all, what treats did the female give to the puppy in the litter when she received the appropriate action from him? What do you do if you are outside or in a position where you do not have any treats? Your dog feels deprived of the reward for doing what was asked of him, and will eventually stop performing. Praise with your hands is always available.

Some dogs will work better and faster with a food (treat) reward than others. Keep in mind that the treat is only going to be of a size that will fit neatly between your thumb and forefinger; a pinch of the treat. The reward should not be an entire treat but a portion of the treat. You want the dog to work and be rewarded for working, not eat a meal. The treats that you give during training should not exceed more than 10 percent of your dog's daily food intake. You may start with treats, but you must wean your dog off them, by alternating a treat with praise. Do not get into a repetitious mode. Mix up the treat and praise so that the dog does not know which one it is going to receive. After a while, eliminate the treat. If the dog shows signs of lapsing, give the treat, but only on occasion. Give him just enough to get him back on track. Eventually, he will not look for the treat and will enjoy just being patted.

The reason I have stayed away from food rewards (treats) is that once the dog has a treat, it feels that it has finished the exercise. Take, for example, an avalanche where a dog was being used to locate persons who were buried. One dog, on finding food buried in the snow, stopped working. It felt that it had accomplished what it should, because the food reward was there. Since learning this, I have stayed away from food rewards.

Praise is the key. Hands are the instruments of praise. If you do this with consistency, you will see that your dog really enjoys being touched when you are accepting his actions. Dogs do not have the ability to touch in the same manner as humans, so being stroked is very pleasing to dogs. They will work hard to get a few pats from you, and they will melt with stroking.

Verbal praise is done with a happy tone in your voice. You must help the dog to understand the difference by letting him hear how happy and excited you are with his actions. Do not get overly excited, as it will cause the dog to lose focus. Just use a voice that has a happy tone to it. Oh, you may think that your neighbors and friends are going to laugh at what you are doing, but in a few short lessons, when they see how well your dog behaves, they will be trying it, probably where you will not be able to see them. Do not let that interfere with training. It's an important part of the praise process.

For example, let us say you are enrolled in a class that is teaching you how to work with your dog. The instructor takes the time to point out the things you are doing wrong, with an explanation and demonstration. Then, when you do it correctly, he praises you by saying, "That's right! Now, you have it. Good work." You feel a level of achievement and acceptance. The pleasant sound of his voice lets you know that he is pleased with what you have done.

Now let us look at the other side. Your instructor is the military type and barks orders. He tells you that you're not doing it right, marches off in front of you saying, "This is how it's supposed to be done," and hands everything back to you. As you begin to come into the groove of working your dog in the manner prescribed, he says, "There you go. That's better."

Which instructor would you choose? The sound of acceptance will win out over any other, and your dog is looking for that acceptance. Get happy when you are working with your dog, and praise him in happy tones.

This chapter may appear short, but that is all it takes. There is not any secret method of dealing with a dog's affection. Praise is the key, and it will work better and faster than any other method when applied properly.

Chapter 14
Training Defined

Before beginning to train your dog, you should know the background of the breed of dog you are going to be working with and his stages of development. You should understand the types and uses of the training equipment if you are to be successful in training your dog.

Basic training, basic obedience, or basic obedience training is the foundation upon which you are going to build. The instructions contained in this book are very basic and can be accomplished by anyone wishing to have a dog with manners.

Manners - the socially correct way of acting; etiquette.

All too often, I am told, "I don't want to show my dog," or "I don't want a lead-and-feed dog," or "I can buy a puppet on a string. I just want my dog to listen to me when I tell him something." These are the same words used when most of us talk to our children—"All I want is for you to listen to me." In order to accomplish these wishes, you must instruct (train) in the ways that you feel are appropriate. You teach (train) your children to say *please* and *thank you* right after they learn to say *Mommy* and *Daddy.* You are proud when a compliment is paid to you for your children's politeness (manners). You have taken the time to train your children in the basics of manners. That is what you are going to do here. You are going to teach the basic manners to your dog. Every dog that has been seen in the Westminster Dog Show has started out with basic training, basic obedience, or manners. If you think of obedience training as working with your dog to improve his manners, you will have the concept of what I am trying to pass on to you.

Dog training is the term used when someone wants to teach a dog to perform a specific action. I have learned through the years that this is not what we are actually doing. What we are doing is teaching a dog to respond to the things he already knows, but to do it when we give him the order to do it. For example, you want your dog to sit. He already knows how to sit, but what you want is for him to sit *on command.* This is a response to a command. This may sound too simple, but it is the truth. Dogs already know how to sit, lie down, walk, run, fetch, jump, and pick up objects. These things are learned before they are six weeks old. If you doubt this, just watch a litter of puppies in order to see what I mean.

You want to have a dog perform the command you give him as a responsive reaction to what he already knows how to do; only now he will do it on command. This is a trained dog, a socially accepted dog, or a dog with manners. Therefore, what we really want is to teach the dog to perform a function when commanded to do so, not how to perform certain functions.

The key to training is consistency and timing. The key to good training is consistency, timing, patience, and love with authority. What most people have trouble with is making the discipline correction. The things I hear are: "I don't want my dog to hate me," or "I want him to protect us but I don't want to make him mean." Now there is a contradiction in terms. If he is going to protect, he will be mean in that mode of response. This does not mean that he will be the killer dog that you have to fear each and every time he is out of his kennel. What it means is that the dog must be able to use the things he has, in order to perform the function you have asked him to do. If he is a protector, he will be taught a switch word that will make him respond from nice and easy to ferocious and fearsome. If you want him to protect, he must be allowed to use his teeth. After all, what good would a protection dog be if he barked, jumped up and down, and just licked an intruder?

I receive requests from people asking me to train their dogs because they are causing problems. More often than not, it's the owners who have created their problems, either by not correcting the dogs or by making an attempt to correct them in the wrong manner. What good does it do to tell your dog to sit three or four times while you wait for him to respond? You must teach with authority. Dogs respect their leader. You must be that leader. If you do not want to be a leader or present yourself as a leader, your dog will become that leader. Then, the next step is to find a behaviorist who can solve your dog's problems.

Most dog owners will listen to what friends say worked for them, or read a few magazine articles on training, then attempt to train their dog. Unfortunately, they usually become frustrated and create more problems than they solve. The trick is to know more than one method of training. I have tried to give you the simplest and most effective ways to train. I like to compare dog training with fishing. If the fish are not biting on worms, try crickets. If that does not work, try minnows. In other words, keep trying until you find what the fish want. The same holds true for training dogs. There is not any *one* method that will work on all dogs. There are many methods of teaching a dog to respond to a given command. Some dogs will cower if you raise your voice too loud. Then there are those that you correct with a collar, and they just look at you as if to say, "Just what do you think you are doing?" There is a middle ground for training any dog. You must find that middle ground and work with it. Most of the time, an owner will decide to train a dog based on his or her experience with one he or she previously owned. When the new dog does not respond to the training method, the owner often decides that the dog is "useless," "stupid," "the worst dog I've ever owned," or "cannot be trained."

I have heard all of the excuses you can imagine, including "I guess I got the dumbest dog in the litter." It is not the dog's fault that you have not taken the time to investigate what can be done to help him understand his training. It is my opinion that your dog should receive the same attention in training that you would give to your child. If you want a child to understand the rules, you must teach him. Sometimes this requires discipline. The same holds true with your dog. If the dog does not understand discipline and reward, you will have an animal that is confused and will try to please you in whatever way he thinks is correct. This is where owners misread their dogs and want to take them to the local shelter. Fortunately, some trainers can notice the problems with owners and correct the actions of their dogs. This is accomplished by having an owner admit that he has to change the way he is dealing with his dog and begin a positive training method. With a positive training method, there must be a positive attitude to training. If you are negative about training, you will have a negatively trained dog that will respond out of fear.

Obedience and loyalty are gained through training. This includes discipline, reward, and love. What good is a dog that responds to your every command, if you never take the time to play with him? Everyone needs some form of entertainment. Even the "boring person" that we so often label will have his own form of entertainment. This is a way of releasing stress, relaxing, and getting your mind off the day-to-day worries. Your dog needs some time to play as well. If he is expected to perform in the manner you wish, he will need some time to play with you and have his own time just to be a dog. When I teach this portion of the class, I get some really strange looks. "Sir, you talk as if the dog were a human being." No, he is not a human being. He is a dog. A dog is a pack animal. Even though we have domesticated them, the instincts are still there. We have instincts and are often told to follow our first instinct. Dogs do that naturally. Then, when they do, we get to a point of complete frustration, and lose control of the situation. Take the time to understand what your dog is doing, and why he is doing the things he does.

There are many books written on training and many different aspects of training. Most of these methods will work on some dogs. Not all methods work on all dogs. You must find the method that will work on your dog and follow it. To teach a dog to sit on command is a common situation. Some owners say how smart their dog is because he responds so rapidly as a puppy. The object is to get him to sit without the treat.

This is the scenario: "My dog would sit as a puppy every time I asked him. Now that he is grown, he will sit only when he wants to." The trick is to use those puppy attitudes to achieve your goal and to expand on them.

Praise is petting your dog and placing your hands on him. Your hands are your dog's favorite treats. Anytime you place your hands on your dog, you are telling him that you are happy with what he is doing.

This same praise mechanism can get owners into trouble. Owners must remember that the hands are for "praise only." Corrections must come by any means other than the hands. To use an example, let us take the dog that jumps up on people. An owner has his dog on a lead, under control, and walks up to greet a friend. As they meet, the dog jumps up to say hello. The owner pulls the dog off, using the lead, and generally saying "No." Then, when the dog is on the ground again, the owner reaches down and praises the dog, saying, "Good boy." This is where the hands can cause trouble. If you pet him now, you are telling him that you approve of his previous action. Then the owner calls a trainer and says, "My dog won't stop jumping on people. I correct him, but he still does it." What has happened is that you have not corrected him properly. Pull him off the person, but do not pet him.

While we are on the subject of correction, I would like to address the overuse of the word "NO." What you should be saying to your dog for jumping up is "OFF." "NO" should be reserved for the harshest command given to your dog. As you begin training with your dog, you will encounter undesirable actions. You will use methods to deter those actions, and you will give a single-word command each time. The one thing that all owners have in common, no matter what breed they own, is the overuse of the word "No." This word slips into the command, and is used with every instruction. "No, get off the sofa." "No, stay off the bed." "No, don't jump on me." "No, don't play with that." "No, stay out of the garbage." The word is used so much that the dog becomes numb to it, and the command ends up without any meaning or authority. It is just as easy to direct the dog with a command word that will stop the action.

Let us take the examples from above. "Get off the sofa - Stay off the bed - Don't jump on me." The one opposing word these actions have in common is "off." Make that the command instead of overusing "No." In the other examples—Do not play with that - Stay out of the garbage—what you really want is the dog to leave those things alone. The proper command here would be "Leave it." Now the dog understands the commands "Off" and "Leave it." Each command has a meaning and a required action. The dog now understands what action is required, because he has an individual command directing him to the desired action.

Save the command "No" for those times when you really need it. When you use the word *no,* use it in such a way as to make the dog believe that the wrath of the "dog god" is about to come down on him. Use it when he has bolted from the house or yard. Use it when he charges your guests. Use it to stop aggressive action. Use it in life-threatening situations, either your dog's life or someone else's. "No" is a great command, but it is overused and misused. Even when dogs tangle in a fight, I <u>will not</u> use the command "NO." In that type of situation, I generally yell "CUT." The "k" sound gets the attention, because the word somehow has the ring of a growl being given by the supreme commander, and gets their attention. At this point, I seize the opportunity to separate them. It is human nature to say the phrase "cut it out" whenever we are annoyed with what is happening.

The first word out of our mouth is "cut," so why not use it to your advantage?

Training can be fun and rewarding. It must be fun for the dog if you intend to succeed. Whether you are working with a dog for the first time or have had some experience with other dogs, you must come to understand that training must be fun. If the training session is not fun for the dog, he will reject your attempts at teaching, and, instead of learning, he will reach a level of frustration. If you are frustrated, your training session will be a disaster. It will cause more setbacks than advances, because the dog's confusion will only add to your frustration. If you continue your attempts at training while you are in this mood, your frustration will eventually turn to anger, and the training session—as well as any bond that you have built with your dog—could be destroyed. You may get your dog to perform the required task, but he will be acting out of fear of your reprisal, rather than wanting to please its master.

You should also realize that your dog might not understand what you want from him on the first few attempts at teaching a new discipline. Do not attempt to teach your dog everything in one day. Be happy having him learn one new thing each week. This may seem to you that it is going to take forever, but by going slowly, you will have a dog that will respond every time you give him a command. Trying to teach too much too soon will only lead to confusion for the dog. Give him time to learn and understand what it is you want him to do. You and the dog will be much happier in the end.

The dog that works to please its master is a happier dog. If the dog is happy, he will help you to be a happier person when you are around him. He will do his best to please you and make you smile, no matter what your mood. Dogs know us better than we know them. They know our moods the minute we approach them. If we give ourselves enough time to try to understand the dog, our lives together will be much more fulfilling.

If you are not feeling well, had a bad day at the office, or you are just not yourself, do not attempt any training with your dog. The dog will sense that you are having a difficult day without your ever saying a word. In its own way, it will attempt to change your attitude, and you will want the dog to perform to your expectations. The two will clash. It is better not to train the dog when you are having a bad day than to destroy what you have built. Accept your feelings, and your dog will accept you.

Another thing to keep in mind is that the lead is just like a telephone line. Whatever your feelings are on your end, it will be felt on the other end. It is as if the lead were a connector to your inner self, which conducts your feelings directly to the dog. On days like these, it is better to let the dog be a dog, and you just enjoy his company. There will be times when a correction must be made, to help the dog understand what action you desire from him, but you must keep in mind that these corrections are performed to assist the dog in performing the proper action. Corrections should only be made for improper action.

Corrections should be defined as: "instructions applied in a physical manner to obtain a positive response." This means that an applied correction does not necessarily inflict pain. It is used only to assist the dog in understanding how you want it to respond to a given command.

If you are having a good training session—that is, everything you do is going well and the dog is responding as if it were reading your mind—you should limit the amount of time spent during this session. It is better to end a session on a good note than to push the dog until it is tired or begins making mistakes. By training in this manner, you will find a dog that wants to learn and is happy while learning a new lesson. Keep your sessions short and fun. Fifteen minutes of positive training is better than any amount of time spent in frustration. If you have the time and you want to train your dog twice a day, you should space your sessions at least four hours apart. By spacing your sessions this far apart, your dog will not tire of training.

There are those who believe the dog must be trained every day or he will forget, and there are others who believe that one lesson is enough for the dog to understand. Either one of these options will cause frustration and confusion. A dog may learn a lesson in one session, but it will not remember the lesson unless it is repeated a number of times. On the other hand, working a dog every day will become boring for the dog, and it will tire of all training.

The method I prefer to use is to work with the dog for two or three days, give him a day off, and then work another two or three days. This break in training seems to keep the dog's attention focused on learning and responding. Take yourself, for example. You probably work five or six days a week and then you get a day off. At some time during the year, you get a vacation, a break from your normal, everyday routine. Your dog needs time off just as you do, and he can use a vacation from training. This helps him keep a positive attitude. Giving your dog a day off does not mean that you do not play with him or use some of the commands he already knows. It means that you do not enter into a formal training regimen for that day. You may give him the commands he knows, and play with him while using those commands, but do not enter into a training session. Let him go for that walk, run and jump around, fetch a ball, or just be a dog.

Play sessions are a required part of training. If you want your dog to respond to you, you and he must form a bond. What better way to form that bond than through play. Your dog will look forward to seeing you, because he knows that you will be paying him some attention and he will get to run around and play. If these play sessions are not utilized, the dog will find a way to entertain himself, and the form of entertainment the dog chooses is generally not the one you find most desirable.

Chapter 15
Training Application and Trainers

D ogs work out problems from instinct and lessons learned. They learn most of their actions and interactions while still in the litter. Their mother will teach them that she is the boss and must be obeyed. The puppies learn from their littermates such things as playing, fighting, hunting, biting, dominance, pain, and teamwork. Dogs are not on the same mental level as humans or learn in the same manner as we do. Humans use logic to learn and to resolve a problem. Dogs learn through trial and error, commonly referred to as *conditioned response.* The dog will attempt to achieve whatever goal it has in mind until it encounters pain or frustration. After a painful experience, the dog will still want to achieve that goal, but it will approach it much more reluctantly than it did in the beginning, and it will look for other ways to succeed. Let me pose a situation that happens with owners of every new puppy.

A new puppy is brought into the house, and this is a playful little ball of fluff that wants to be close to you every minute. You are the new pack (family), and he wants to be a part of it. As you walk around, the puppy gets underfoot. You will try not to step on him, because you do not want to hurt him. This will go on for hours and sometimes for days. You are walking as if your legs cannot go in one direction any longer, and the puppy is always in the place where you want to put your foot. Eventually, it happens! You think that it is okay to move from your present position, and when you do, you step on the puppy's foot. He will yelp and cry, and you will run to console your puppy, saying, "I'm sorry, but I told you not to get in the way. Maybe now you will stay out from under my feet." Surprisingly, the puppy will stay out from under your feet or at least keep his distance when you are moving around. Not because you have explained to him that he needs to be out of the way, but because he experienced pain from his action and learned to move when those big feet are in motion. You did not mean to step on the puppy, but you did. Unknowingly, you have taught the puppy a very valuable lesson.

Unfortunately, the puppy suffered pain in learning this lesson, but it is a lesson that it will not forget. Now when you call your puppy, it approaches you with caution, watches your feet, and is aware of its surroundings until it is sure that it will not be hurt again. Here you have a lesson that is learned rapidly, but not without setbacks. The once-carefree puppy that wanted to be close to you all the time is now very reluctant to approach you with the vigor that it had in the past. This lesson can be taught without the puppy being stepped on, and it will produce the same effect; however, it does take time. The difference is the pain factor. The puppy learned rapidly from pain, but it became much more cautious of its owners. It will overcome the reluctance to approach, but not without reassurance from the owner.

When you give a command, the dog must understand what action is required from that command. You must teach the action, incorporate the command with the action, and repeat both the action and the command as many times as necessary for the dog to understand. As you teach the dog the action and the command, you will use the lead or leash to show the dog what correction will be used if the command is not followed. After the dog understands the command and action, it should respond positively when the command is given. If it does not, you will use the prescribed correction to achieve the response required. The intensity of the correction may need to be increased, or the manner in which the correction is given may need to be adjusted in order to get the dog to respond properly.

Keep in mind that the correction is made only after the dog is given three seconds to respond to the command. If it does not respond within three seconds, give the command again followed by an immediate correction, and lend whatever assistance is needed to have the dog perform. After doing this three times, give the command and allow the dog the opportunity (three seconds) to respond without a correction. Repeat this until you reach a positive result.

Do not try to rush through the exercise. Rushing to achieve results will only serve to confuse the dog and frustrate you when he does not perform.

If you want your dog to look sharp, you must make him look sharp. If you accept a sloppy performance, then you are to blame, not the dog. Your dog is trying to please you. If you accept sloppiness, the dog thinks you are pleased with this. If you show him that you are not going to accept anything other than what you want, your dog will respond to your wishes.

It is important that the correction not be applied in a brutal manner. Consider the correction to be an "attention-getter" rather than an instrument of brutality. Do not correct your dog so hard that it cowers in fear. Harsh corrections administered regularly will break the dog's spirit. You do not want to break his spirit, but you do want him to respect you and respond to your commands.

You will encounter sessions that will frustrate you, and you will think that either the dog cannot learn or you cannot perform the exercise. You can do it. Take your time. Some dogs learn more rapidly than others. The key ingredient is to practice patience, timing, consistency, and motivation in every training session, and you will achieve much faster results.

PATIENCE—Dogs can try your patience and wear you down. It sometimes becomes a test of wills. You must succeed. You must win the battle.

TIMING—If corrections are not made in a timely manner, the dog will not understand why it is being given a correction. Keep the three-second rule uppermost in your mind, and ensure that all corrections come within three seconds of the command.

CONSISTENCY—You must be consistent with your praise, your commands, and your corrections. The more consistent you are with your dog, the easier it will be to train him.

MOTIVATION—In any type of training you do, you must find what motivates the dog to perform the feat you are attempting. He must think he is doing something that pleases you, but he must also enjoy it.

The amount of time spent training your dog is just as important as the lesson you are trying to teach. I recommend spending fifteen minutes on any new exercise, then include that exercise into your dog's program. In the beginning, your program will be short, but it will grow as you introduce other disciplines. It is important to mix up the sequence of the program so that the dog does not respond to a prescribed routine. In addition to the training session, the number of times a session is repeated is also important. You should work your dog on a new exercise for approximately three days, and then give him a day off. Some owners believe that their dog will forget if he is not worked every day, but the dog will be relieved for the rest from the continuous regimen. You will find that by giving him a break, he will not become bored with training. Then, on the next lesson after being rested, he will be willing to work and please you. If you wish to work with your dog more than once each day, be sure that there is a four-hour break between training sessions. Repeating a training session in less than four hours could cause some frustration on the part of the dog.

All dogs reach a training plateau where they decide they are not going to oblige you or your wishes any longer. It usually occurs at around the fifth week of training. If this should happen, continue on your lesson. You may become frustrated and the dog may act as if he has never heard any of the commands before, but it will pass in about three days. Just be patient, and do not give up.

When the dog has accomplished all of the exercises that you intend to teach him, you should work him on the entire routine at least once a week after training is complete. This will keep him sharp, and he will not forget the commands and exercises.

I have observed dogs that were trained by children who just wanted their dog to do a trick. I have seen things such as shake hands, roll over, dance, sit up, beg, and speak. These were all done by being consistent and patient. Keep in mind that these feats were not done by a professional trainer, but by children. The point is, you *can* train your dog. Most dogs will learn if you will take the time to teach them.

For example, in my kennel I have sixteen dogs. The lesson I am going to tell you was performed with five dogs, and as the dog numbers began to increase, each new dog learned the lesson. My kennel is approximately 250 feet from my driveway and positioned behind and to one side of my house. Whenever anyone would enter the driveway, the dogs would begin barking their arrival. With the single command "Quiet," I can stop all of the dogs from barking. Most people think this is amazing. It is not amazing, it is conditioning.

To accomplish this, I would give the single command word, "Quiet." I would fire a blank pistol after the command in order to make a noise that would distract them. I would do this out of their sight, so that the sound would not appear as coming from me. This would change their focus of attention to the direction of the noise. I would again command, "Quiet." After approximately seven to ten days, the dogs understood the command "Quiet" and responded by not barking. At night, I would turn on a light, walk to the kennel, spray

141

each dog with a water hose, and command "Quiet." The dogs became so conditioned to the chain of events that I can now shine a flashlight out of my bedroom window, without getting out of bed, and they will stop barking. The responsiveness was taught through conditioning and the use of patience, timing, consistency, and motivation. They didn't like the idea of being wet, and became conditioned to the fact that when the light came on at night, they must stop barking.

My search-and-rescue dog would eliminate on command. If a dog can be taught to use the bathroom when given a command, surely you can teach the fundamentals of obedience. All you need is patience, timing, consistency, and motivation.

One thing that I am frequently asked is whether a dog is too old to be trained. This question usually comes from someone who has reached a point of frustration with a dog that is about two years old. In truth, any dog can be trained at almost any age. Dogs that are ten years old are capable of learning new things. The hardest problem is to eliminate the bad habits that formed over those past ten years. This usually requires a change in habit for the owner as well as the dog.

Think about some of the habits that humans have developed over the years of their lives. Let us use nail-biting as an example. One day, you decide that you want to change that habit. It requires a great deal of willpower and consistency to make the change. If you remind yourself each day that you want fingernails, the bad habit goes away, and the nails begin to grow. A new, positive habit takes the place of the negative habit, and now you must care for the nails and keep them trimmed. You are very proud of your accomplishment, and are happy when others notice that you have stopped biting your nails.

The same techniques are used when training an older dog. You must be consistent, persistent, and you must make the changes. Doing this will end the bad habit, and new ones will begin. You will not achieve overnight success when trying to break a bad habit. It may take six to eight weeks of consistent training to break it. If you have not had success in eight weeks, do not despair. Just keep up the positive training and reinforcement, and you will see the change eventually. If the bad habit continues without any improvement, either you are overlooking the cause of the problem or your correction is not meaningful. At that point, you should seek professional help.

My Dog Knows He Did Wrong

Some owners say that their dog misbehaves and knows when he has done something wrong. My question to them is, how can he know? He is just being a dog.

Their explanation usually sounds like this: When I come into the house and see what he has done, I just look at him, ask him what he has done, and he will lower his head and slink away. He knows that he did something wrong, or he would be happy to see me. These are not the actions of a dog that knows he has done something wrong, but the *reaction* of a dog whose owner unknowingly trained it to react to body language and voice tones. I have had many discussions about this, and when I say I can prove that they have trained their dog, they are amazed.

What usually happens is that the dog does something that you consider wrong, such shredding and scattering the newspaper all over the floor. You walk into the house, see the paper, and ask, "What did you do?" in a very stern voice, grab the dog by his collar, take him over to the paper, spank him, and tell him he is a bad dog. Your actions are a means of teaching the dog to respond. The tone of voice and body language are perceived as a warning of what is to come, and the dog will slink away. He has been conditioned to the body language and the tone of your voice, but not the words. To prove this, I generally have the client enter the house, look at their dog in the same manner as if it had done something wrong, approach the dog and say, "I love you." They are surprised to see their dog slink away from them.

If having your newspaper thrown all over the floor is not what you want, you should either remove the paper from access or place the dog in his crate while you are away. I know you are saying that he never does it when you are at home, and he only does it to spite you. This is not true. He does not do it when you are at home because he has you to entertain and distract him from other fun things. He has you to keep him company.

A dog could be lying down in a corner, minding his manners and relaxing, and his owner will say, "Hey buddy, had a hard day?" The dog will get up and come to him. The dog was lying down, behaving himself, and the owner has now gotten him up. They cannot understand why the dog just did not lie there. After all, he was not called, he was just spoken to. The tone of voice, body language, and the attention attracts the dog. He heard you talking to him and he wants to be with you. He does not understand your questioning, only the fact that you are trying to get his attention. If you do not want him by you, then let him lie there without disturbing him.

Dogs are not spiteful or cunning enough to make plans to ruin your day. Dogs are just being dogs. You may have to make some changes in the way you are accustomed to doing things, in order to correct your dog's behavior.

Next time you find your shoes pulled out, think before you react. Should the dog have been allowed to roam the entire house while you were out? Did you allow him to chew on or play with shoes when he was a puppy? Does he know the difference between good shoes and old ones? How can he? They both have the same smell. Most of the time, all it takes is just thinking through what has happened and how to make it better. Establish some rules for your dog and yourself, and stick to them. Do not make excuses for either of you.

There is a three- to five-second rule that applies to all training and conditioning. If you do not see your dog misbehaving, then punishing him is fruitless. If you see him misbehaving and cannot get to him within three to five seconds to make a correction, then it is too late. He will not understand why he is being punished. Corrections for behavior problems and training must be performed within three to five seconds, in order for them to be effective.

TRAINERS

If you feel that you need to seek the assistance of a professional trainer, then select one as you would a doctor. Ask friends or veterinarians for the names of trainers. Look in the local newspaper and phone book, or go online and search for one closest to you.

Call the trainer and discuss the problem you are having, or what it is you want to achieve. If there is a simple solution to the problem, most trainers will tell you what to do over the phone. If they feel you need to attend training sessions, they will advise you as to when to attend. Before signing up for training, inquire as to the method of training, qualifications, experience with your breed, and go observe some of their training sessions.

There are many good trainers, each with his or her own personality and method of training, and there are numerous methods to solve a particular problem. Any good trainer will readily admit that there are methods that work on some dogs but not others. Trainers must be flexible enough to see when the method they are using on a particular dog is not working, and change that method for the sake of the dog. Continually using a method that is not working will only serve to instill fear, confusion, frustration, or submissive behavior in a dog. Flexibility is the key ingredient for a good trainer.

You must feel comfortable with your trainer and his techniques. You must trust him and his knowledge. After all, he will be handling your dog. You must feel relaxed in his classroom environment, and he must make his directions and explanations understood by all. Do not be afraid to ask questions, and do not be afraid of making a mistake. You are there paying him, and you need to know what to do and how to do it successfully. If you do not understand his method of training, you must ask. If you feel intimidated, confused, are not making progress, or feel that you cannot convey your position, then it is time to find another trainer.

Here is an example of trainers and opinions that you may want to remember. If five trainers were presented with a training problem, placed in a room, and allowed one hour to find a solution, at the end of the hour, there would be six solutions, and someone would probably have a black eye. Each of the six solutions would be very viable, workable solutions that would probably work on some dogs. What you have are five knowledgeable trainers with differing personalities, methods, and opinions. Combining all of that knowledge would bring about a sixth solution. You have to be the judge and decide which trainer makes you feel the most comfortable while being the most effective in training both you and your dog.

Chapter 16
The Controlled Walk

This is your starting point or foundation block on which to build. As you begin training, your dog should be positioned at your **left** side, and you will use your left hand to make the majority of the corrections, when needed. This may seem awkward at first, but you will become accustomed to having your dog in this position within a few days.

The controlled walk is an exercise in which your dog is made to pay attention to you, your body movements, and direction of travel. Do not confuse this exercise with the "heel" command. You are not teaching your dog to heel at this time, but you are teaching him to pay attention to you and your desired direction of travel. This is one of the most important steps in gaining control of your dog. Gaining your dog's attention and respect are paramount.

In a classroom environment, students learn this exercise and are sent home to practice. At the next session, the owners are remarking about how much differently their dogs are behaving. Many say that this first lesson has seemed to calm their dogs a great deal. They find their dogs paying much more attention to them, and they no longer have to drag their dog or have their dog drag them down the street. I like this exercise for these reasons: 1) It gives the handler a lot of confidence; 2) It brings the dog under control rapidly; 3) Your dog begins to respect you as a leader. When this exercise is performed properly, the dog will focus all of his attention on the handler, and—probably for the first time—the dog views his owner/handler as a leader.

This exercise should be performed with the dog wearing his training collar. When a dog is first placed on the lead for a walk, he will do one of the following: 1) take off running with you being dragged behind; 2) try to escape the control of the lead by lying down and refusing to move; 3) fight and/or bite at the lead; or 4) try to run between your legs while cowering. These are all common problems and are easily resolved.

Once the collar and lead are connected, you should not talk to the dog. Do not give any commands, verbal praise, petting, or reassuring comments. If you are frustrated, remain quiet. Keep your frustrations non-verbal. Your dog should not hear any sound coming from you at this time. He must be taught to observe your body language (movements) and your choice of direction without any verbal direction or comment from you.

Let us start with the dragger. This dog refuses to walk, fights/bites at the lead, or insists on lying on the ground. First, try coaxing the dog into walking toward you while he is wearing the lead. Talk to him and encourage him to move in your direction. If he gets up and starts to come to you, do not get all excited. Just keep happy tones and allow him to move toward you, and when he is within two feet of you, start walking backward, and stop talking. This will have the dog trying to reach you, and you will be moving away slowly. Once the dog is reassured that no harm is going to come to him, you may begin walking him in the proper manner. If a dog refuses to move at all, even after being reassured by the above exercise, you will have to use a more forceful approach, otherwise the dog will be training you.

At this point, your dog has already gained some control over you by making you stop your actions when he lies down, so you will have to show your leadership.

Begin by walking in a straight line with the dog dragging behind. Do not walk and stop to look back, but begin walking with conviction. Pick out a point on the horizon and start walking toward it. This sounds like a horrible thing, but the majority of dogs will not allow you to drag them more than five feet before getting to their feet and walking. This can be compared to the child who decides she is not going to walk. She will throw herself to the ground and refuse to move. Usually, the parent will take one hand and drag her, causing her to stand, or the parent will pick her up and carry her. You will not be carrying your dog around, so the only answer is to demonstrate your conviction and begin walking. Once standing, he will walk with some reluctance, but he will be walking. Do not jerk the lead, especially if this is a puppy less than six months of age. You must remember that there is no talking to the dog at this point. He would not walk when you were talking in pleasing tones, so now there will be no talking.

This may sound harsh, but you are showing the dog that you have assumed control. When your dog realizes that he is losing this battle, he will give up and begin walking. There may be some lagging (staying behind you) at first, but eventually he will walk at your side. He has to gain confidence that all is well, even though he is being guided around. Once the confidence is there, he will walk willingly with you. You are teaching him that you have assumed control of the leader position and that you must be obeyed.

Do not talk to the dog, do not give any commands, and *do not wait for the dog.* Once you begin, pick out an object on the horizon and walk straight for it. Do not talk, hesitate, or stop until you get there. When you reach your chosen point, turn to the right, choose another object, and walk straight to it. You must walk rapidly and with conviction. You are not out for a stroll; you are training your dog. Step out with lively steps and at a speed that would be the midpoint between walking and jogging. This will have you walking at a speed just above your normal walk. If the dog thinks you are going to hesitate or wait for him, you will have trouble getting him to obey you. He must perceive you as the leader; therefore, you must walk with conviction and confidence. This exercise should not last any longer than five minutes. If your dog is still fighting the lead or is refusing to walk willingly, do not console him. Take him to get some water, and release him from the exercise. Do not try to accomplish too much in one session, and don't chastise the dog for not complying on his first try at this. It is new to him and he is reluctant to give up control to you. When released from this exercise, spend some time playing with your dog. He is confused by the event that just took place and will be unsure of your actions. Give him a chance to settle down and regain his confidence. This is similar to the manner in which instructions were handed out in the litter. He was removed from the litter, allowed to do whatever he wanted within the limits of his boundaries, and now you are telling him that he no longer has that option. Be patient; it will happen.

The dog that tries to get between your feet and cower is a very submissive dog. Do not make any harsh corrections. Walk without speaking. If the dog tries to get between your legs while you are walking, kick your heels in an upward motion, behind you, as you walk. Do not kick so hard that you will hurt the dog, but make it uncomfortable and awkward for him to get between your feet. Move them upward in a rapid motion. This type of walk may feel a little uncomfortable and unnatural to you, but it will create an area of discomfort for the dog. He will move out from between your legs in fear of being hit by your feet kicking backwards. You might hit your dog when you first start kicking up your heels, but you will not be doing it with a force that will hurt him. You want to move your feet just enough to make that area an uncomfortable place to be. Once the dog moves from between your feet, you must gently guide him to the left side. Do not drag the dog to your left side. Put enough continuous pressure on the lead to cause the dog to move to the left side while you are walking. Gentle, continuous tugs on the lead will help the dog to understand that there is no pressure from the lead when he walks beside you, only a constant tugging (nagging) when he does not.

Now, here comes the puller. This dog decides that his walk is going to be a race, and off he goes, dragging you behind him while you are yelling for him to slow down. You swear that you heard an announcement: "Gentlemen, start your doggies," and it is off to the races while you are being dragged behind. This problem is much easier to correct. As you begin your walk, the dog will take off out in front of you. What you will have to do is create slack in the lead. The best way to do this is to bring the lead as close to your body as possible then place your arm holding the lead straight out and pull it back to you as rapidly as you can. At the same time, change the direction you are walking. When he realizes that you have changed direction and he is being pulled, he will change direction also, and will probably come running past you. The instant he passes you, pull on the lead and change direction again. When he realizes you have changed again, so will he. Continue this each time he passes by you. Change direction, sharply and with conviction. If he goes north, you go south. If he goes east, you go west. Try to make 180-degree turns to the right. Do not say anything to the dog during this time. Do not give any commands, talk, yell, chastise, or praise. Say nothing. The dog will go off expecting you to follow, because he thinks he is the leader and in charge. Whenever you change direction, he gets to the end of the lead, and, "bang," you are going in another direction. Now he has to catch up with you. Once he gets there, he decides he is going to lead. Off he goes in front of you again. Bang, you change direction sharply, repeatedly. Each time he gets to the end of the leash, you suddenly decide to go in the opposite direction. Make these changes with conviction and confidence. Your dog has to trust you as the leader. If you are not confident that you are in charge and walk with conviction, he will not respect you. After a few of these rapid changes in direction, the dog will run alongside and look up at you. What the dog is thinking is, "I'll have to watch this guy. He's a complete idiot and has no sense of direction." When he looks up at you, praise him by saying, "Good boy, watch me."

With this type of dog, it usually takes between thirty seconds and one minute to convince him that you are in charge. Now you have gained control over the dog. Once you have his attention, you may make smoother turns, to keep his attention focused on you. The most important thing in this entire exercise is *walking with conviction and silence.* Do not talk to the dog at all. When the exercise is completed (ten to fifteen minutes), you may praise and talk to him. Again, take him to get a drink of water, release him from the exercise, and spend a few minutes playing with him. Within two days of this exercise, your dog will be paying much more attention to you when you have the lead on him, and those walks will begin to be more pleasurable for both of you.

Continue working with the dog on this exercise for five days. Do not cheat yourself or your dog. If you want to work your dog more than once a day, be sure there is a four-hour break between training sessions. Do not overwork your dog. To work him in less than four-hour intervals or to work him beyond the point of learning will make him tire of the training, and he will rebel.

Releasing your dog from an exercise is a formality that is often omitted. When the dog is no longer in a formal training session, and it's okay for him to run around and play, give him a command word so that he will understand that work time is over. Whenever I finish a training session, I replace the training collar with the flat collar and give the command "free dog." When giving this command, I allow the dog the freedom to run, play, and do whatever he enjoys.

It just lets them know that they are back in control of themselves, and are allowed to go about the business of being a dog. As you progress in your training, he will understand that when you give him commands and directions, he must obey, no matter what collar he is wearing.

Chapter 17
Watch Me

I n the previous chapter, Controlled Walk, you will recall telling the
dog to "watch me" when he began to look up at you. Use of this
command during that period ensures that the dog's attention is
focused on you and your movements, and builds the dog's confidence
level. He learns that watching you is fun and rewarding. He does not
get many corrections, because he now has his attention focused on you
rather than his surroundings. The dog took the initiative to look up
at you so he would be aware of your movements and direction. It is
at this point that you want to maintain that confidence and attention.
Whenever the dog looks at you during an exercise or just wants to give
you that look to see what you are doing, reinforce it by giving him the
command "watch me." Praise him for looking at you, and command
again—i.e., "Good boy, watch me."

"Watch me" is the command you will use to have your dog look
directly into your face. Teaching your dog this command will aid in
keeping him focused on you. You will have all of his attention focused

on you and on what you are doing, thereby helping to give him a foothold into learning a new feat. It enables you to instruct him while he is concentrating on you, and helps him learn faster and easier.

I try to get students to use this command early in their training, because somewhere in the training process, they are going to hear themselves repeatedly saying to the dog, "Pay attention." If you teach the "watch me" command at the start, you will already have his attention when you want it, and you will not have to remind him to "pay attention."

Stand in front of your dog, bend over him, and cradle his face between the palms of your hands so that he is looking directly at your face. As you do this, command him to "watch me." When your dog is looking at you, do not look directly into his eyes, but instead look over his head or down at his nose. Staring directly into the eyes of some dogs may be considered a challenge, and you do not want to challenge your dog. He may turn away the first few times you do this, but continue to talk to him, saying, "Watch me." Do not yell or allow yourself to become frustrated with him. This is something new to him, and he is not sure of what it is you want. Reassure him in very soothing tones while repeating, "Watch me, good boy, watch me."

If he decides that this is not what he wants to do and begins backing up, do not fight him, but hold steady pressure on the lead. You are trying to gain his trust and attention. Any wrestling with the dog at this point could cause a setback in training. You want his trust and confidence in you. Simply walk away from the exercise while holding the lead, and, as he walks up to you again, repeat the command "Watch me."

If the dog does not look up at you while you are walking him, reach down with your left hand and gently tap the bridge of his nose with two fingers and repeat the "watch me" command. Continue this whenever you are working with your dog until he will look at you without turning away.

You should add this into each practice session, no matter which lesson you are working on. Once he understands, you will be able to have him focus on you, no matter what lesson you are teaching. I can assure you that you will be glad you taught him this command when you are heeling him and he is looking directly at you, waiting for the next command.

Chapter 18
Sit

"Sit" is one of the things that the dog already knows how to do. What you want now is to have him sit when you give him the command. This is not a difficult thing to teach, but it does take patience. Whether you are training a puppy or an adult dog, you will accomplish this exercise by following these instructions.

Start by placing the lead on the collar. For a puppy less than four months of age, you will be using a flat collar. Dogs more than four months of age will be using the training collar. Ensure that the collar is placed on the dog in the proper manner. Review the section on equipment for proper placement. Remain in a standing position with your dog on your left side, and with your right hand, hold the lead approximately ten to twelve inches from the collar and directly over the dog's head. Form a "U" with your thumb and middle finger of your left hand. Turn your left hand over and place it on top of your dog's rear end, just in front of the rear leg muscles. These pressure points will help you to guide your dog into the desired position. Give the command "Sit." Do not say anything other than the command, and say it only once. Take up the slack in the lead with your right hand, causing the lead and collar to become taut. Using the thumb and middle finger of your left hand, squeeze inward with your fingers and press downward firmly with your hand, placing the dog into a sitting position as you simultaneously raise the lead straight upward over the dog's head. As the dog sits, release the pressure on both the rear end and the lead. Praise the dog by petting him and saying, "Good boy. Good sit." This praise should not last more than three seconds. If you spend too much time praising him, he will think it is time to play. So do not overdo the praise. You will repeat this exercise until the dog maintains this position when placed in it.

If you find yourself having trouble using the lead at this time, you may grab the collar at the back of the dog's neck with your right hand and apply the upward pressure.

If your dog gets up immediately, which is usual, command him to sit again, and repeat the procedure. Continue doing this until the dog sits and does not get up. You may have to make him sit ten times, or you may have to do it thirty times until he gets the idea. This may take some time, but he will catch on much faster with you placing your hands on him and guiding him into position. Eventually, he will be sitting before you can make a move. This lesson should not last more than ten to fifteen minutes. If you have not accomplished the exercise at the end of the lesson, stop the exercise and begin again the next day.

Once you have accomplished the "sit," do not bend over to give your dog his instructions. Remain in an upright position and give the commands. Bending or hovering over your dog could be interpreted as bowing to the dog or a display of wanting to play. This could lead to other improper behavior. In the submissive dog, the problem will generally present itself with submissive urination. In the more dominant dog, it could be read as your being an equal and lead to a challenge of your authority. If your dog thinks that you will submit to him, he will begin to ignore you and your commands. Your dog can hear you when you are standing, and you will be able to make a lead correction from this position, thereby maintaining your authority without being a threat.

From the standing position, give the command for your dog to sit. If he does not sit within three seconds of the first command, you must issue the correction. Give the command again, followed immediately by the correction. The correction is performed like popping a whip. You will allow about two to three inches of slack in the lead, and then pull upward rapidly and with enough force to cause the collar to tighten. You will then release the pressure on the collar equally as fast. This is called a "pop" correction. This correction is to get his attention and remind him of the lesson you have previously taught him. The release will be just as rapid as the correction. Remember, you do not want to hang the dog, just get his attention. The "pop and release" should take less than the tick of a clock, one-fifth of a second, to perform. The correction must be straight up over the dog's head, and slightly forward. Do not pull the lead across your body when you impose this correction. Pulling the lead across your body will cause the dog to sit and/or lean against your leg, or he will sit facing you from the side.

When the correction is applied for the first time, your dog may panic and attempt to back away. This is a normal reaction. Just be patient with him and allow him to figure out what just happened to him. Once he realizes that when he sits, there is no correction, he will no longer resist the collar. If he does not sit after the correction, hold the lead straight up and place him in position with your left hand.

When he sits, you must praise him. Do that by petting him and saying, "Good boy. Good sit." This praise should not last longer than three seconds. Take a few steps forward, stop, and command him to sit again. If he does not sit, correct him. If it appears that he is only going to sit when you place him in position, your correction is not firm enough. Increase the intensity of the correction, but be sure not to go above the "yelp" correction.

When he sits, make certain that he is in the proper position. He should be in the sit position, facing the same direction as you, with his right shoulder even with your left leg. Do not accept his sitting facing you from any direction while at your side. He may look up at you, but he has to sit straight. If he sits crooked, straighten him up. If you accept sloppiness at the foundation of your training, you are going to have sloppiness all the way through. Stop his sloppiness and yours in the beginning, and you will be much happier with your dog's performance in the end.

If he continues sitting in front of you, do not praise him for sitting. Walk directly into him, take one or two steps, and turn to the left as you stop. Give the command to sit as you turn toward him. Continue this until he gets the idea that each time he sits in front of you, you are going to walk into him, but when he sits at your side, you are pleased with his action. Praise him only when he performs it correctly. If he sits, but is not in the proper position, then he has not done it correctly.

If your dog should sit and then get up after a couple of seconds, do it again and again and again. Continue this procedure until he sits on command without the correction and understands that he has three seconds to respond before he will be given the correction.

Knowing that he will receive a correction for not responding to this command, your dog will instinctively attempt to beat you to the correction. You will give the command, and your dog's bottom will fall to the ground. He is trying to accomplish the exercise before you can correct him. There will be times when he does not respond because of inattention. All you have to do is apply the correction to remind him that you are still in charge and have not lost control.

Do not get into the bad habit of repeating the command. If you continue to repeat the command, correct, repeat and correct, you are teaching your dog that he does not have to sit until the second or third command is given. Give one command, allow him three seconds to respond, and give a correction if it is needed. You want him to respond to the first and only command. Bite your tongue if you repeat a command. If you bite hard enough, you will not repeat it again. Get the idea?

Anytime you see your dog sit on his own, for whatever reason, you should praise him for sitting. Even if you are not within reach to pet him, you should give him the verbal praise, "Good sit." He will hear the praise in a satisfying tone of approval and begin to associate the command with the action. You will be surprised at how rapidly they catch on when you sound pleased at what they have just done. This verbal praise should also come within three seconds of the action. He may get up when he hears your voice, but ignore the action. You did not command him to sit, so he does not have to remain seated. The only time you will force him into position is during a formal training session where you have complete control.

Treat Training

Many dogs have been taught to sit by offering them a treat. Owners are satisfied that their dogs respond to this offer and feel they have done a good job. I feel that they have done a great injustice to their dog. The dog will work for food, but what happens when you do not have a pocketful of treats? Treat training is okay as a starter, but you must wean them off the treats and have them accept praise. Some dogs will work better because of their food drive, but when there is no offer of food, they will completely ignore you. What I hear is this: "Well, if I had some treats, he would do anything I ask him." Okay, so what does he do when you do not have any treats? Do not answer that. I already know the answer.

When using treats in training, the most common mistake made is to reward the dog with too much of the treat. Whatever type of treat you are using should be given in small amounts. The reward should not be any bigger than one that could be hidden between your finger and thumb. You do not want the treats used in training to replace a meal.

Standing in front of your dog, allow him to sniff what you are holding. This will get his attention. Hold the dog's rear in place with one hand so that he cannot back up, and give the command to "sit." Move the hand with the treat toward the dog and just over his nose. As he begins to raise his head to get the treat, move your hand higher and toward the rear of the dog. As he raises his head, put pressure on the rear so that he assumes a sitting position. When he sits, you may give him the treat and praise him for sitting. Alternate giving the treat and praise with praise and not giving a treat. When he begins to show signs that he understands the command, you should reduce the number of times he is given the treat. Start by mixing treat and praise so that there is not any type of pattern that the dog could recognize. You do not want him to know when he is going to get the treat. Continue this until he no longer looks for the treat. When he completes an exercise that meets with your approval, you may give him a treat at the end of the exercise. Eventually, you will have a dog that will perform a complete routine for you without any treats until you release him from his exercise. You want a dog that will respond to you and not expect to be fed each time he performs. He will expect praise, and he deserves that, so give it to him.

Let us look at the circus performer. He commands the dog to walk on a large ball. The dog does so, people applaud, and he has given a reward. When the same dog comes out to walk on his hind legs, he is given nothing. The trainer makes a hand gesture as if he was giving a reward but does not. The dog continues to do his job without any begging. If you watch closely, you will see that the trainer will hold the treat in his fingers, but he will not give it to the dog. This is called "baiting." It is used to have a dog perform with the idea that he will be rewarded with the treat, but he does not get it until the very end of the performance. In my opinion, "baiting" is nothing more than "teasing." Some owners use this method in the show ring to keep their dog's attention focused on them. What the dog is focused on is the treat, and not the handler. I have mixed feelings about the use of treats and do not use them in obedience training.

Whichever method you choose to use, you should work on this exercise for five days before continuing on to the next exercise. You will work with your dog for fifteen minutes on this exercise, then you will add the controlled walk and sit for another five minutes. You are beginning to build a working program for your dog. You should be working with your dog a minimum of five times each week to ensure that he learns and understands the exercise before going on to another exercise.

If you are having a bad practice session, or if you have not succeeded by the end of the learning session, have the dog perform something that he does well. It does not matter what it is, as long as he performs it with success. You always want to end your sessions with a successful finish. This keeps the dog happy and upbeat, knowing that you will be happy with his performance, and he will try to please you again at the next practice.

Chapter 19
Heel

Assuming that you have mastered the controlled walk and sit, you may now add the *heel* to your exercises. If you are still having trouble with your dog sitting at your side on command, do not start this exercise. Wait until he performs the "sit" command properly. Advancing before he has accomplished the prior lesson will only serve to confuse him and frustrate you.

Before any training of the heel command begins, you must understand what this command means and how it is performed. When I conduct classes, I always ask for my clients to give me their interpretation of this command. A number of them will say, "It's when you call your dog to come and walk with you." That is close, but incorrect. Heeling is to have your dog walking with you at your left side. This is where he should be positioned whenever he is walking with you. Calling him to come to you is not any part of the heel exercise. The "come" command will be covered in another lesson.

Heeling your dog, having him walk when you do, involves three speeds of movement. The three speeds of heeling are slow, normal, and fast.

The **slow** walk is probably the way you normally walk at this time. When you walk a dog in this manner, you allow him to "window-shop." In other words, he is walking at a speed slow enough for him to put his nose to the ground and examine all of the different smells in the area, and his curiosity drives him to investigate it further. This is the reason most people have trouble getting their dogs to walk beside them. You will use the slow walk, but not until you have mastered the heel at the "normal" speed.

The **normal** walk is a pace about two steps faster than the speed you would normally walk. It is at a brisk pace, but not a jog or run. If it normally requires you to take eight steps to travel twenty feet, then the **normal** walk would be at a speed that would require six steps to travel the same twenty feet. At this pace, the dog does not have time to window-shop, because you are moving at a speed where he has to focus on your moveme☺nts. He must focus on you, because he does not know when you are going to stop or make a turn, or what is going to happen next. This speed will keep him attentive to where you are going and what you are doing, and he does not have time to "window-shop."

The **fast** walk is at a speed where you are almost in a jogging pace. Your dog is walking along at a very fast pace, but not running. He will be in a rapid walk, with his feet keeping a rhythmic beat. This is the walk you will see when they are showing off the dogs in the ring. You will see the handler moving in long, rapid strides, and the dog will be walking very rapidly, but not running. If the dog is allowed to run during this exercise, he will think you are playing and begin to jump up while you are walking. If this should happen, slow down a bit. Find the level that will keep him moving at a fast pace, but not running or playing.

When you are training him to heel, always start out with the **normal** pace. The speeds, slow and fast, are added only after the dog understands what is expected of him when he is commanded to heel.

The proper **heel** position is having your dog at your **left** side and his shoulder parallel with your **left** leg. He should maintain this position whenever he is at your side, whether sitting or in motion.

As you begin, your dog should be sitting at your **left** side. Place the loop handle of the lead over the thumb of your <u>right</u> hand. Hold the lead with your <u>left</u> hand, allowing two to three inches of slack to hang from the collar. Gather the remainder of the lead and place it in your right hand or let it hang down in front of you. Place your left forearm against your left hip, with your hand pointed slightly outward. With the lead in this position, you will have enough slack so that, should a correction be required, you will be able to do it without a lot of fuss. Remember, **timing** is very important in a correction. The correction, if needed, must come at the proper time, and just enough to get his attention. If the lead is too tight, the dog will feel threatened by the tight collar and will be reluctant to walk with you. If there is too much slack, he will go about doing what he wants, making it hard for you to correct him. If you have to gather in the slack prior to making a correction, it is too late. The correction will be applied, but the dog will not understand why he was corrected. You must find the medium of the two.

Prior to any movement on your part, all of the verbal signals must be expressed. You will say your dog's name, and give the command prior to any movement of your body. Moving before you give the command could cause your dog to receive a correction, however slight, for not meeting a command he had not yet received.

Prior to any forward motion, you must pick out an object in the distance, focus on that object, and begin to heel your dog by heading straight for that object. If you look down to see what the dog is doing or watch him while you are heeling, he will lose confidence in you as a leader and begin doing what he wants.

Now you are ready to start. You will say your dog's name and give the verbal command, "Heel." Then you will step out with your **left** foot. You must always step out with your **left** foot whenever you want your dog to move along with you. Your voice, his name, and the command are his primary signals to move. The movement from your **left** foot is his secondary signal to move. As you step out, the lead will begin to tighten, and your dog should move with you. If he has not moved by the time your right foot leaves the ground, it will cause your left hand to be pulled downward. Snap your hand back into position and this will signal the dog to move. Once you have him moving, you must keep him at your side. Do not let him **lag** (walk behind you) or **forge** (pull ahead of you). You must keep him walking at your side and about six inches away from your leg. Do not allow him lean on you or attempt to keep you from walking a straight line. Remedies for this follow this section.

After you have walked thirty to fifty feet, you will stop and command him to sit. This requires a bit of timing. Whenever you are ready to stop, you should slow down your pace, take two slower steps to help your dog see that a change is taking place, and give the command to sit. This will help him to stay at your side instead of being out of position in front of you when you stop. The slowing steps will signal him that a change is taking place and allow him to regulate his speed, and prepare for the change.

Try this demonstration with someone in your family. Ask them to pretend to be your dog, and they must respond to the "heel" command. Have them stand on your left side, take their hand in yours, and say, "Heel." Begin walking at the normal pace for about fifty feet. Without giving any signal or saying a word, abruptly stop walking. You will see that your helper is now standing about two steps in front of you. Do the exercise again, only this time take the two slowing steps before you stop. Your helper will recognize a change of pace and stop directly alongside of you. The same thing will happen with your dog when you give this visual signal. He is trying to please you, but if you do not give him a signal, he will not understand that you intend to stop.

You do not want to teach your dog any bad habits, so use the slowing step method to avoid the common problem of having the dog sit in front and to the side of you, looking up at you. When you stop, have both feet together, command "Sit," and pull upward on the lead immediately. If he does not sit, make the correction for sitting. Do not make this correction too harsh, as this will cause the dog to back up and sit behind you, or he will begin fighting you for authority. Once he is sitting in the proper position, you may praise him. You are trying to impress upon him that each time you stop, and your feet are together without any movement, he should sit. This is the "automatic sit." Once learned, whenever you stop heeling, he should sit automatically without any command or signal. This takes time and practice. Continue heeling and stopping in this manner for the next two days. He should get the idea that every time your left foot moves, he should move, and when your feet come together, he should sit.

You are going to have to make some turns at some time during this exercise. When you do, try to make the turn wide and to the right. You want the dog to learn what he is supposed to be doing while he is walking at your side. To teach him how he should turn at this time may cause him some confusion. Just make wide right turns for now. You will be performing other turns that will be taught in a later chapter.

After the second day of heeling exercises, you should start **faking** a step with your **right** foot. With your dog at your **left** side in his proper position, you should step out on your **right** foot, but do not allow your **left** foot to move. If your dog gets up when you move your **right** foot, pull him back to a sitting position immediately. Do not wait for the dog to get up and begin moving around. As soon as he attempts to move from his sitting position, pull him back to that position. Do not say anything to the dog, but just have him sit in his position. Continue to make the **fake** step with your **right** foot until you can do it three times in succession without any movement from your dog. When you are certain he remains sitting with this movement, give the command to "heel" and step out on your **left** foot. The reason for making the fake step with your right foot is to prepare your dog for the "stay"

169

command. This **fake step** helps him to understand that he moves when the left foot moves, and he does not move when the right moves. This may make you look foolish, but you will be happy later. Besides, in my opinion, if you do not feel foolish about what you are doing, you probably are not doing it correctly.

When the dog is consistently heeling alongside of you, try changing your pace. Switch to a slower walk, back to a normal walk, then to fast, and back to normal. Always start out and end up walking at the **normal** pace. Do not try to stop your dog while you are in the fast pace. To do this would cause your dog to stop ahead of you, out of position, and cause him to be confused. After all, you did not give any slowing signals.

When your dog is performing the heel at all three speeds, you should include this with the other exercises. The lessons learned prior to this are now included with this one. You are building a series of exercises that will be combined into a single performance. Work on an exercise for ten to fifteen minutes, and then incorporate all previously learned exercises into a final performance.

At this point, your dog should be doing a controlled walk, heel, and sit. The controlled walk is now a part of the heel exercise, and the sit that you taught previously is now the stop portion of your heel command. When you take him out to practice an exercise, if you give him his commands and he does it properly on the first attempt, STOP training. Give him a few minutes to just walk around, and then try again. If he is successful again, your training session is completed. To continue exercising after he has performed well will only create boredom and confusion. If he has performed perfectly, how can you expect him to improve on it? You will want and expect him to perform to that level again, and he will tire of the exercise. Continuing will only cause him confusion. You will become frustrated that he will not do it again, the same way he did, and the battle is on between you and the dog. All of your lessons will be wasted. If you have trouble completing the exercise, have him perform something he does well. End your exercise on a good note. Let the dog think he was successful.

This will keep him coming back to learn and will prevent him from wanting to run away from you when it is time to work.

Heeling Problems

Forging—If your dog continues to forge ahead of you while you are heeling, make a series of small corrections until he returns to your side at the heel position. These corrections are simply repeated pulls used to nag him, and are not hard corrections. It will serve to slow him down so that he is alongside of you. Once he is alongside, you must stop nagging him.

Lagging—The same nagging correction used for forging is used for lagging. Nag the dog forward until he catches up and is alongside of you. Once he is alongside of you, you must stop nagging him.

Another method of correction for lagging and teaching your dog to heel, which has given good results, is the lead droop. With the dog in a sitting position on your left side, drape the lead so that it is below your left knee. Pull it taut, and hold the remainder on your right side at waist level. With the lead in this position, command "Heel," and step out with your left foot. As your left leg moves forward, it will put pressure on the dog's collar, and he will move along with you. As he begins to heel, give him some slack and continue with the exercise. He may be reluctant to walk in this manner at first, but be persistent. In a few days, he will get the idea and stay at your side. Once this is accomplished, you will not have to drape yourself in the lead.

Leaning—If your dog insists on leaning against you when he is sitting, it may be due to your making an improper correction. Ensure that the correction you make for sitting is straight above the dog's head, and that you are not pulling the lead across your body. If you are correcting properly and he still insists on leaning, step sideways away from him and allow him to fall over. He will tire of this and start sitting properly. If he is leaning against you when he is heeling, try holding the lead out a little farther from your body as you heel your dog, or make turns into him.

Guiding (or walking into you)—The dog, at this point, is trying to regain control. If he can guide you where he wants to go, he is successful. Do not let him succeed. When he begins to guide, you should walk directly into him. Making sharp left turns will keep him off your leg. If he continues to try to guide you, try crossing your feet while you are walking. Cross your left foot with your right, and vice versa. This crazy walk you did as a child will cause the dog to move away and watch your feet. He will do this to prevent being injured, and by doing so, will provide you with the desired space.

Window-shopping—Sniffing the ground is something a dog loves to do. It tells him all kinds of things. These are interesting things to him, but none of them pertains to training. If he insists on holding his head to the ground after he is given the heel command, you may try moving the collar up higher on his neck. To do this, move the collar up the dog's neck so that it is behind the jawbone and rising directly behind his ears. Connect the lead to the "dead" ring, the collar ring that doesn't move, and heel your dog while holding his head up. You will be surprised by the better performance. Since he can no longer see the ground, he will raise his paws higher to prevent tripping. That is how handlers get their show dogs to achieve their high-stepping gait, and your dog will start walking with the same type of gait.

One of the things I do with my students is to have them walk their dog in an area where I have placed pieces of hot dog on the ground. I will also hide some under a piece of paper or an object. If you can get your dog to heel through all of this without losing his focus, you have accomplished the lesson. Your dog is giving you his undivided attention.

It should be understood that, once trained, your dog will not be in a formal heeling pattern each time you take him for a leisurely stroll. Allow him to look about and check out his surroundings, but when you're ready to return home or must move rapidly, give the command "heel," and he will return to his place at your side.

Chapter 20
Stay

D o you remember that fake step you have been taking in the heeling section? Well, now you are going to put it to work. If you have been practicing the fake step properly, you should not have much difficulty with this exercise.

With your dog sitting at the heel position, place the palm of your right hand in front of your dog's face, and command him to "stay." Move your hand back to your side, and step away from him on your **right** foot. You will always leave your dog on your **right** foot. As you step away, approximately three feet in front of him, turn and face him. Wait ten seconds, and return to your dog by circling him to the right. Continue around the dog until you reach the heel position. When you have returned to the heel position, you must wait approximately five seconds before praising the dog. When you praise the dog, make sure to repeat the command, i.e., "Good boy, good stay." Praising the dog immediately upon your return to the heel position and not waiting the five seconds will cause him to anticipate the praise, and he will get up from the stay as you return.

If your dog insists on getting up and moving as you are leaving him after the stay command, you should "bop" him in the nose with the palm of your right hand and command him again to stay. Do not hit the dog on top of his nose, but ensure that the "bop" is directly into the nose. This should not be a hard correction, but one with enough force to move his head backward one inch. Your hand will touch his nose long enough for it to get wet. You want him to feel your hand, but you do not want to hurt him. At the most, you will have a wet palm, and your dog will not move. If it appears that he will not listen to this command with the "bop" correction, the next step is a lead correction. You will place your right hand in front of his face, and command, "Stay." As you bop him in the nose with your right hand, you will pop the lead straight back toward his rear. Keep in mind that this pop will not go any further in intensity than the nag you used when he was lagging or forging.

If he gets up or moves toward you while you are standing in front of him, raise the lead rapidly, high into the air, so that his end of the lead taps him under the chin. Repeat the command, "Stay." If he continues to come to you, give him a heel command and place him back in the exact same spot he was in when you put him in the stay. If he is allowed to move to the spot he desires and then sits, he is not listening to the command and is telling you he wants to sit in this new spot. You are in charge now, and he must stay where you place him. This exercise works with the same principles as the "sit" exercise. If he gets up twenty times, put him in place twenty-one times. Continue doing the exercise until he sits and stays in one spot facing you for a minimum of ten seconds. After ten seconds of staying, return to your dog by circling him to the right until you return to the heel position.

If he gets up as you start to circle him, return him to the sitting position and facing the same direction as when you began the exercise. Do not allow him to move while you are walking around him. Some dogs will get up as you pass by them and try to walk with you. The reason for this is that they see you going around them and lose sight of you at a point on their left side. When you leave the sight of the dog, he believes you have vanished. He is concerned about where you went, and he will get up to find you. Do not let him get up. If he continues to get up as you start to circle him, try this: As you get to the dog's left side, but in a position where he can still see you, stop your movement for a second or two. Allow him to relax, and then step over his back quickly so that you suddenly appear on his right side in the heel position. This will reassure the dog that you have not disappeared. Once he is sure that you are not leaving him, he will allow you to circle him. When you have circled him and are in the heel position, wait five seconds before praising him with "Good boy, good stay." Next, heel him two steps forward and have him sit. Now you should praise him again and release him from the exercise if you are finished, or move on to repeating the exercise.

Practice this for ten minutes each day for the next five days. At the end of this lesson, include it in your dog's program. Your program will now consist of a sitting, watch me, heel with an automatic sit, and stay. Mix up the commands so that they are not always in the same order. In other words, start with a heel no matter what he is doing. Place him in a sitting position, and then heel him again. Then sit and stay, and so on. Just keep mixing it up so he knows the commands and not the routine. Your lessons should last approximately ten minutes. Your lesson and program combined should last twenty minutes.

When you have accomplished the "sit/stay" for ten seconds and the return, begin adding distractions and distance. You want your dog to stay, no matter what is going on around him. If he likes a ball, bounce it while he is in the stay position. If he gets up, put him back in the same spot as when you first commanded him to stay. Once he accepts the distraction, you must increase your distance by moving backward a few feet and adding a few more seconds of staying time. Continue this until you are at the end of your lead. If he is stubborn, you must be even more stubborn. You will want your dog to sit and stay for at least one minute before going on to the next lesson. If you desire him to stay longer, that is fine, but you must achieve the one-minute mark before continuing. When using distractions, try moving about, like jumping, dancing, and singing, and just fooling around. If he gets up, put him back. This sounds silly, but your dog must become accustomed to staying, no matter what you are doing.

When you have achieved that magic one-minute mark, take him where there are many distractions. One place I send my students is the entrance of a shopping center or mini-mall. You will still have control with the lead, but the distractions are tremendous. When he will stay, even with all of the distractions, take him to a safe place and start walking away to a position where he cannot see you. If possible, position yourself so that you can see him. A mirror strategically placed will allow you to do this. If he attempts to get up, correct him first with a voice command, and if that does not work, go back to him and place him in the stay again.

Another way of correcting him from out of sight is to place a long line on his collar and have him sit next to a tree or post. Pass the line around the object so that the dog is on one side and the line is around the other side. Place the other end of the line where you intend to hide. If he attempts to get up while you are out of sight, make the correction by pulling the line. This will have the same effect as if you were standing next to him, but now he is being reminded to stay when he thinks no one is there.

Chapter 21
Come

T he majority of the problems I see with dogs that do not come when called are not the dog's problem, but one that has been created by the owner. I know—I have just accused you of creating a problem in your dog. Read on and you will see what I mean.

Here is the scenario, and it is okay to laugh at yourself if this has happened to you. First, you call the dog in your normal tone, expecting a response. "Fido, come here." You get a response, but it is more like a look from the dog that seems to say, "Are you talking to me?" He continues doing what he wants, totally ignoring you, and you decide to move closer to him. Why? I do not know, because he heard you the first time you called, but you figure that if you get closer, maybe he will come. Then you call again, "Fido, come!" Fido looks at you and assumes a stance that tells you he is not going to come but wants you to come to him, and you oblige. What a smart dog! He has got a human trained to move in just one short lesson. You move toward him, calling just a bit louder, "Fido, come here!" Fido looks back but continues to move away. You move closer, but you are not moving much faster. You call him and give a louder command in a much sterner voice, as if that would make a difference. "FIDO, COME!" Fido thinks, "Come? You mean you want me to come over there where you are? Why? It is more fun to run around having you chase me." You are now trying to catch the dog and yelling, *"Fido, you son of a blue-eyed mongrel, you're dead if I ever get my hands on you again!"* Well, that was a waste of time and energy, because you're not going to kill him, and you will just be happy that you finally have him when you do get him.

You have just entered into a dog's favorite game of CHASE. You are calling the dog, moving closer and closer, until you are running around chasing him, trying to catch him. You are calling his name with a few obscenities and yelling about his family tree. The dog's focus is on play. You have initiated the game of chase, you are running around, and to the dog, all that yelling is your way of barking. Hey, this is some fun, huh? Okay, I guess it is not any fun at all, but you can make it fun. Since the dog wants to play chase, why do not you do all that same yelling, calling, shouting, clapping your hands, and running *away* from the dog? Chase is the same game, whether you are chasing him, or he is chasing you. Turn the tables on the dog. You are still barking (calling the dog) but now you are running away. He has to follow if he wants the game to continue. Dogs love this game so much, that they will usually stop, turn, and look at you, and think, "Hey, new game!" and begin to come after you. If he begins to run away, stop chasing him, clap your hands, call his name, and run away in the opposite direction, yelling, "Come!" Most people are pleasantly surprised to see their dog stop dead in his tracks and start to chase them. We have now made the command a fun game.

You will not want to be running around the neighborhood yelling, with your dog following you, so you must help him understand what you really want.

Before you begin training with the "come" command, some things must be understood and followed without exception. NEVER call your dog to you for a correction. If he is doing something wrong, go to him to make the correction. Do not call him to you. Calling a dog to you for a correction will only have the dog very wary of coming to you. It is common for all of us to avoid danger, and calling your dog to correct him gives him the idea that you have become dangerous. This will make him avoid coming to you. If you were to call someone's name, ask them to come to you, then smacked them in the head when they got there, how many times do you think they would come to you when you called them? Not many more. So why would your dog be so foolish as to come to you when he knows you are going to punish him? He believes that he is being punished for responding to the call. You believe that you called him and corrected him for what he had done. To the dog, you called him and corrected him for coming. He will begin to stay out of your reach so that you cannot do it again, or he will slink to the ground and crawl submissively toward you.

Whenever your dog is called and he comes, he must receive praise. Put your hands on him and emit happy tones. It does not make any difference that you came home and found the mink coat chewed to shreds and it is lying in his bed. You did not catch him in the act, so you are wasting your time with corrections. You are only releasing your frustrations and alienating your dog. Besides, why did you leave him alone with full run of the house? It is not his fault!

As a puppy, he would come when he was called, but now he only comes to you when he feels like it. As a puppy, he was growing and his attention was focused on you, because you were the leader of this pack. As he began to grow, the types of games you were playing have changed, and the amounts of time spent with him have diminished. He is not a puppy any longer, and you do not play with him as much as you did. Now he has to look for another way to entertain himself. You do not want to play after a hard day's work, but the dog does. So, to help him understand that you are happy and willing to accept his attentions, you must pet, praise, and spend some time with him. Do you remember how the puppy came to you? He was happy, bouncing, full of energy, and looking for fun, and you made a point of playing with him.

The sound of the word "come" is very similar sounding to the word "fun." When you think you have just about had it with your dog, think about these words. You want him to "come," so make it "fun." You can even use the word "fun" in substitution of the command "come," and your dog will respond to it. Okay, you got the picture; now let us teach the dog.

Begin this lesson by placing your dog in a sit/stay. Walk to the full extension of your six-foot lead, turn, and face your dog. Call him by saying his name first and then the command "come," i.e., "Fido, come." As the command "come" leaves your mouth, pull the lead toward you while taking up the slack in your lead, similar to pulling in a fish, until the dog is standing directly in front of you. When he arrives, command him into a sitting position, and praise him for coming. "Good boy, good come." Give him a minute to relax, and then do it again. Do this about three or four times.

Be sure that when called, the dog comes and sits directly in front and between your feet without touching you. If you have trouble making him sit squarely in front of you, try having him come to you through a makeshift aisle. Place chairs in a row forming an aisle, and have him come to you via the aisle. Do not give him any room to get around you or sit crookedly. Praise him for coming and sitting squarely. He may be hesitant at first, but he will do this exercise. When he is performing well, remove the chairs and perform the exercise. If he begins to sit crookedly again, return to the aisle exercise until he sits squarely in front each time he is called. Continue until he performs without the use of the aisle.

The next step in this training is to remind him that this command is "FUN." You will place him in the sit/stay and go to the end of your lead. You are going to call him, "Fido, come," but now you are going to begin backing up as fast as you can. Continue backing until the dog catches up to you. Command him to "sit," and praise him for coming. "Good boy, good come." When the dog begins to understand the game a little better, he will be jumping out to get to you before you can back up more than three or four steps. This is an indicator that the dog is having fun. Now, instead of backing up when you call him, you will turn around and run away. This will excite the dog, and he will run after you. After a few short paces, stop running, turn to the dog, and have him sit. Praise him for coming. Give him lots of praise. You want him to know that you are pleased with what he has done, and you must demonstrate that pleasure.

Now that he is coming to you on the short lead, begin calling him while you have him out for a walk. When he is looking around and not paying any attention to you, call his name and command "Come." If he does not respond, reel him in, repeating the command, and praise him when he is next to you. Continue this practice until he responds, no matter what his interests.

The next phase of this training involves a long line. You will need a section of line that should not be any bigger in diameter than one-eighth inch, and approximately twenty-five feet long. I find that using pull cord, the type used on chainsaws, works the best, and it is extremely strong. Tie a snap on one end of the line, and fashion a loop in the other end. Snap fittings may be purchased at the local hardware store. Snap the line on the dog's collar, and wrap the loop end around your hand. Be careful when working with this line. A pulling dog can cause a nasty cut. Use this line as you would your lead; only allow the dog to travel the full extent of it. When he is at the end of the line, call him to "come." If he does not respond, reel him in. Vary the distances on this line, and do not always call him from the same distance. Never let him know when he is going to be called. Once he understands that he must come, no matter what he is doing, and that you can get him with that line, he will come to you. Since there is twenty-five feet of line, the dog can feel the line on him and knows that you have control of him. At this point, you will want to switch over to some nylon fishing line. This is light, and the dog cannot feel it. Now when you call, you still have control, but the dog cannot figure out how you were able to stop him and make him come.

Keep in mind that you must be in control and in charge. He must never be given a chance to make any mistakes or disobey during this lesson. You call, he comes, period.

Timing is the most important thing. You do not give your dog a chance to think about coming before you tug on him. You should command and tug. After a few of these lessons, he will be jumping up and running to get to you when you call.

Be certain that you work with your dog around lots of distractions when teaching the "come" command. You want his coming to you to be the most important thing in his life. No matter what he wants to do, he must come to you when he is called.

Do not test your dog to see if he will come to you while he is off lead. You must be certain that the dog understands the command and that he will respond in a manner that brings him from one place to you quickly and directly. If your dog is walking slowly when he is called, he must be made to come faster. The turn-and-run method should improve this.

Once he is responding consistently without hesitation, you may attempt some off-lead work. Start with the sit-stay, walk away about fifteen feet, and call him. If he responds to this positively, perform the same test with distractions. When he is responding to this test, increase the distance. Your dog must respond to this command in the face of distractions before you may increase the distance. Do not increase the distance too much, or the dog may not respond to the command. Increase your distance in increments of five feet.

If your dog should decide that he is not going to come to you or he should run off in another direction when he is called, go to him if you can, and bring him back to the spot where you called him. Stop training in this manner and return to the lead or line until your dog understands that he must come each time he is called.

If your dog is one of those overly exuberant dogs that just wants to come to you and knock you down, try this: When you call and he begins coming, position yourself so that you are facing him. Square yourself up with him, and just prior to his arrival, poke out one knee just far enough for him to see the movement, and he will stop charging. When he stops, give him a "sit" command, and then praise him. Your knee changes the shape of what he is used to seeing, and the sudden change in formation confuses him enough that he will stop running as a caution to prevent injury to himself.

Praise him for both coming and sitting, i.e., "Good boy, good come, good sit." Once he realizes that he must sit before any praise is given, he will automatically come to you when he is called, sit in front of you, and look up, waiting for that praise. Be sure you give it to him, and do not be stingy. He did what you wanted; now love him for it.

As with any lesson or command being taught, if the dog provides the action on his own, praise him for doing it. In other words, if your dog just walks up to you and sits, praise him and remind him of what he just did. "Good boy, good come, good sit." This will help him to associate the command "come and sit" with his action, and it will help you with your training lessons.

Chapter 22
The Finish

*T*he finish, seen primarily at dog shows, is the action that the dog performs after being recalled (come). On command, the dog will get up from a sitting position, circle the handler, return to the heel position, and sit. This exercise is used to place the dog back at the heel position so that it will be ready to perform the next feat. It is a handy exercise for getting the dog out of your path also.

The finish is not hard to teach, but it takes a little patience and coordination. To begin teaching the finish, your dog must come when called and sit squarely in front of you. He cannot be allowed to sit to either side of you. If he sits a little to your right, it will not hurt, but squarely in front is better. Once that is accomplished, the finish can be taught.

After your dog is called (come) and sits in front of you, you will give him a command to move to the heel position. The command may be "Finish," "About," "Return," or any command that will not interfere with any of the other commands your dog understands.

Amazingly, your dog already knows how to perform this action. You have to learn. Along with giving him a new command word, you will have to learn the footwork and hand signal to help the dog understand what it is that you want him to do.

First, choose a word that you will use to have the dog perform the "finish." I will use the word "about" in the following examples. Next, have your dog sit in front of you in the same position as the recall. You may even practice the recall while teaching him. If you decide that is what you want to do, do not go into the "finish" directly after he is called. Praise him for coming and sitting squarely. Do not praise him too much, or he will lose focus of the lesson and he will think he has finished working and want to play. Pause for about fifteen seconds after the recall before going into the "finish" exercise.

By incorporating the command "Heel" along with the command "About," he will respond much quicker to the new command and the action associated with that command. When he is sitting in front, place the lead in your right hand, give the command "About," followed by the command "Heel." You should pause for one second between the commands. At the same time as you give the "heel" command, take a large step *backward* with your *right* foot only. This will cause the dog to get up and begin to move in the same direction that you have stepped. The reason for this movement is due to the leg closest to him moving in his forward direction and his being given the command to "heel" in that direction. As he begins to walk by you, take a large step *forward* with your *right* foot as far forward as you can reach without losing balance. As you step forward, pass the lead around your back and into your left hand. As you are changing hands with the lead, step out with your *left* foot until it is even with your right foot, and stop all motion. Your dog should circle behind you, assume the heel position, and sit. If he does not sit, give him the correction for sitting. If your dog does not move or seems confused by all the movements, simply guide him through the movement that you desire. That is, to move from the "sit" position, cross behind you, and return to a sitting position at your left side. If your dog sits behind you, take an extra step forward to reinforce his proper position and have him sit.

After a few of these lessons, you will notice your dog beginning his motion after the command "About." When that happens, eliminate the command "Heel." He will know what to do when the command "About" is given, and you will not need the redundant commands any longer.

Continue practicing this lesson in the above fashion for about one week. At the end of the week, begin using your empty right hand to signal him into the "finish." For example, command him to "about," move your right hand alongside the right side of your body, and point it backward. Your dog should begin the motion to perform the finish. Do not move your feet unless the dog does not understand or needs to be guided. If that should happen, make the same motions to guide him through the steps and back to the "heel" position. Simply give him a tug with the lead and pass it behind your back into your left hand. Your dog should walk around you and into the heel position. After this is practiced for a few days, he will get the idea and begin the movement when he is given this command.

If your dog is reluctant to begin his movements as you step rearward on your right foot, try this: Place the lead around the back of your right leg at knee level, and hold it in your left hand. As you step backward, the dog will be pulled into the motion. Then gather up the lead at your left side as you are moving forward, and your dog will be there.

Caution! You must insist that your dog come, then sit in front of you and wait for the next command. If this lesson is taught to follow the "sit in front" too soon after he arrives, he will get into the habit of anticipating your command to "finish." When called to "come," he will begin running past your right side and assuming the heel position. Be sure to make him wait in the front position before going into the "finish" exercise.

Chapter 23
Turns and Figure Eights

It is time to stop walking up and down and start making some turns. In this chapter, you will learn how to make turns that will signal your dog of your intentions. This will enable him to turn with you smoothly, instead of bumping into you or you bumping into him.

Let us look at some of the signals we give during the course of a day. While you are driving along in your car, you come to a place where you will make a turn. Before making the turn, you turn on your signal indicator (blinker), or you give a hand signal to alert the person behind you of your intentions. If you are trying to catch a bus or taxi, you raise your hand and wave to get the driver's attention. Your hand waving frantically in the air is a signal that you would like for him to stop. In baseball, the catcher gives a signal to the pitcher. Both the pitcher and the catcher know what type of pitch is to be thrown and where the ball should be caught. The batter is going to try to hit the ball, but he does not get any signals. He has to guess what kind of pitch is coming and try to hit the ball. In football, the quarterback calls out signals to ten men on his team, so that they all know what to do at precisely the same instant. The other team, hopefully, does not know the signal.

You see, we are giving signals in everything we do. When you start making turns with your dog, you need to give him a signal so he will know your intentions. I will explain what signals you are going to give to your dog so that you may make right, left, and about turns without being tangled up with the dog.

Walking your dog, as you know it, is going to change temporarily. You will feel awkward in the beginning, but it will become commonplace while training your dog. You will be making exaggerated movements and shifts in your body weight to help your dog read your intentions. You will not have to perform this awkward walk after your dog understands your body language. You will be giving him strong signals to help him recognize the change in directions. These strong signals and exaggerated movements will be eliminated when the dog is able to read your slightest movement and direction changes. You will be giving signals to your dog that he will understand, and it will become a pleasure to walk with him.

When walking your dog or making turns, you should try to keep your eyes fixed on something in the distance and *avoid looking down at the dog.* You can see your dog without moving your head to look at him. You will also learn to feel your dog's presence by the way the lead feels in your hands. This is important for you and the dog. If the dog does not feel that you are confident in what you are doing, he will attempt to take charge of the situation. You must show him that you know what you are doing, and that he must follow your judgment.

Do you remember when you were a child, and you would perform the crazy walk of crossing your feet over one another? Well, you are going to do it again, only not continually. In order to exaggerate your body movement when turning, you will be crossing your feet one over the other.

Crossover Steps—This method of walking makes you look ridiculous, but it is helpful in making your dog read your body language and prevent him from leaning into you.

As a child, you probably walked like this as a joke, so it will not be too strange to you. As you are walking, cross your right foot over the left, then cross your left foot over the right. Each step causes an exaggerated body movement. Your dog will think you have totally lost your mind, and in his attempt to stay with you, he will move outward but remain at your side. This exercise will help to keep him from leaning against you while you are heeling him. He cannot get close to you, because you are weaving as you are walking. Do not be embarrassed when performing this exercise. Those who are laughing at you today will be amazed at how well your dog performs for you at a later date.

Right Turn—When turning to the right, your dog has to move through the turn much faster in order to keep up with you. As you turn, the space needed for his turn becomes wider than yours, so you must give him a signal that he is to hurry and keep up with you in order to make the turn smoothly.

First, let us concentrate on the footwork. When you begin a right turn, cross your left foot over your right in a sweeping motion. Your left foot will be crossed over your right foot and it will be pointing to your right. Follow this motion by moving your right foot so that it is pointing in the same direction as your left, and continue walking in that direction. You have just made a ninety-degree turn to the right.

You will note that, as you pass your left foot over your right, you begin to lean in the same direction. Crossing your feet over one another exaggerates the shift in your body weight, and it gives a strong signal of your intentions to your dog.

In addition to the footwork, you must use the lead to hurry the dog through the turn. As you begin to turn, pull the lead forward to have him hurry into the right turn. This will force him to stay at your side and move along with you in a very fluid motion. When you are making this turn, do not watch or wait for the dog. It is his job to catch up with you and remain at the heel position. Do you remember that lead-wrapping exercise for lagging while heeling? If you pull your lead tightly around your body as you make the right turn, your dog will be forced to pick up speed and stay with you.

It is commonplace for people to look down at their dog as they are making a turn, and they usually end up creating a circular pattern and making a wider turn than desired. Be certain that you make sharp turns and not wide, circling turns. A turn should be ninety degrees opposite from the direction you were heading.

Left Turn—The left turn is a little trickier to accomplish, because you now have to make the dog move out of your way. As you turn left, your dog will be at your side and directly in your path. You must give him a signal that will have him slow down and stay out of the way.

You will give him similar foot signals as the right turn, only in the opposite direction with an added movement. Start with the right foot crossing over the left, and placed directly in the path of your dog, followed by your left foot. This will exaggerate your movement to the left, but there is one difference: The dog is in the way. In order to make him understand that he must move out of the way or slow down when you turn to the left, you will have to give another signal. In addition to moving the left foot into the left turn, you must raise your knee so that it butts against your dog's face or shoulders. This will cause him to move backward or slow down his pace in order to get out of your way. You do not want to kick the dog. You want to bump into him so that he understands that he is in the way. You should do this without hesitation while completing your turn and forward motion.

As you begin the left turn, pull backward on the lead slightly to slow the dog down from his heeling gait. This will also give the dog an indication that you are turning left and that you want him to be out of the way.

If you own a small dog whose head or shoulders are not even with your knee, you may use your shin or foot to move the dog from your path. Instead of bringing your knee up to meet the dog, use your left foot or shin to butt the dog out of the way. Remember that you are teaching your dog to move out of your way, and not using him as a football to kick field goals. Just make him move.

After a few days of practice, your dog will begin to understand the right and left turns. He will notice your body movement as you begin to make the turn, and you will not have to do those exaggerated movements any longer.

About Turns—The about turn is a term used to have you turn 180 degrees from the direction you are heading. In the military, the term is *about face.*

Start with **right about turns**, by turning 180 degrees to the right. Your dog will have to hurry along to keep up with you. When you make the turn, do not wait for the dog. Make the turn, continue walking without hesitation, and hurry him back into the heel position. Walk a little distance and make the turn again. Once you are certain that your dog understands the right about turn, begin mixing the right turn and the right about turn. This will help him to pay attention to your footwork and body language.

Next, you will perform the **left about turn** by turning 180 degrees to the left, and it will require an extra step. When you turn 180 degrees to the left, you will be standing on top of your dog. To avoid this, you will make the left about turn by placing your right foot slightly to the left and then turning your body the rest of the way to complete the 180 degrees. In other words, your right foot will cross over your left foot before you initiate the left about turn sequence. By doing this, you are placed out and away from your dog, so that you may make the turn smoothly and not trip over him or become tangled in the lead. This turn may take a little more practice than the right about, but it is an effective method to gain your dog's attention, and eliminate his leaning against you.

Figure Eights—The figure eight is performed by walking your dog around two objects. The objects may be chairs, plants, traffic cones, people, etc. Place the two objects approximately ten feet apart. Begin by standing between the two objects, facing away from them, with your dog in a sitting position. When you are ready to begin, give the command, "Heel," and turn toward the object to your left. Circle the first object completely, and pass between the two objects. Next, circle the second object to the right and pass between the two objects again. Stay close to the objects so that the dog has to make hard left and right turns. You will be making figure eights between the two objects. This exercise will help the dog to understand the different turns, stay out of your path, and pay attention to your body language.

Spirals—I find this exercise to be very effective; however, if you get dizzy easily, I do not recommend that you do these. Start by heeling your dog into a turn and making a large circle. With each completion of the circle, move closer to the center. When you reach a point where you are just spinning around, start to move out, and make bigger circles gradually. When you are making bigger circles, about ten to fifteen feet in diameter, heel your dog into a straight line for about fifteen feet, and stop. Praise your dog. Performing the spiral will help you and your dog understand the methods needed in making turns.

Again, if you are the type of person who gets dizzy easily, do not perform this exercise. It can make some people nauseated and force them to lose their balance. We want to train the dog to make turns, not wonder why you are lying on the ground. For those who get a little dizzy and still want to do this exercise, try changing directions. If you are turning to the right, or are coming out of the right spiral and begin to feel dizzy, immediately begin a left spiral for two turns. This will cause the fluid in your head to level off and end the dizzy feeling. Do the opposite for right spirals.

Chapter 24
Down

When approached by a more dominant dog, the lesser of the two will submit to the authority by lying down and attempting to lick the mouth of this leader. Teaching your dog to lie down on command can be accomplished, but you must be patient and persistent. Because the down position is the most submissive position, your dog will be reluctant to do it when you first attempt to teach it to him. You are expecting him to lie down because you have given a command, but he is unsure of his safety and cannot understand why he must do this.

All dogs know how to lie down, and do so when it is convenient for them. They will observe their surroundings and circle before lying down. They want to be certain it is safe for them, and will check all around them, including the ground on which they will lie. Take notice of the dog when he lies down of his own accord. He will always face the direction of perceived danger. When you place him in the down position, he has to rely on your decision that he will be safe. You are telling him that he must obey you, regardless of what he perceives.

When he does this, he is accepting your judgment and putting his trust in your decision.

There are a number of ways to teach your dog to lie down. One is to kneel in front of him and pull his front paws forward while keeping them on the ground, and commanding, "Down." When he is down, praise him. When you release the paws, he will probably get up, and you will have to get him and start over. Another method is to use a food treat placed between your thumb and finger. Keep one hand on his back, placing pressure in a downward direction. The hand holding the treat will pass in front of the dog's nose and then move outward and toward the ground. As the dog reaches for the treat, you force him into the down position while commanding him "Down." Once he is down, you may give him the treat and praise him. Still another method is to kneel beside your dog while he is in a sitting position, give the command "Down," and pass your arm or hand under his body, moving both front paws out in front of him. You should be holding him from moving forward, while putting a downward pressure on him. Praise him when he is down. This is a good method for teaching a puppy.

All of these methods work, but all require you to kneel down beside your dog to begin teaching him. By kneeling down, you are placed on the same level as the dog, and it will take longer to teach him, because he will believe that you are equal to him and he does not have to do what you want. Then, when he understands what you want, you have to make the transition to having him perform while you are standing. I believe this method serves to confuse the dog by the time you're ready to stand and command him down. After all, you were kneeling beside him when you taught him, and now he believes you are to kneel beside him when you command him to lie down. Now you have to make him understand that you are not going to kneel down beside him and that he has to lie down while you are standing. Why not just start in the standing position?

Whether your dog is standing or sitting, he can be taught the "down" command. To do this, you will allow your lead to hang down from the collar, creating a big loop in the lead. Place your left foot on the lead and give the "down" command. After giving the command, pull the lead upward, allowing it to pass under your foot. This motion will cause the dog's head to move toward the ground. As his head moves downward, he will resist the pressure that is drawing him to the ground. Continue moving the lead, even if it requires some of the chain to pass under your foot. When his head is on the ground, hold him there. If he resists going down, just hold your position and he will lie down on his own to remove the pressure. If your dog fights the down position, do not despair. Just keep your foot on the lead and allow him to calm down. Keeping your foot on the lead holds his head downward. He will soon realize that he cannot see anything and will lie down so that he can. If he continues to struggle, observe in which direction he is leaning. Push him in that direction so that he falls over. Do not concern yourself with his position at this time. All you want from him is to understand that he must lie down when he is given this command. If he is on his side, back, or whatever position, it is okay, as long as he is down. Once he understands the down command, he will assume the proper position. For now, you just want him to understand that he must lie down when he hears this command. Once he is in the down position, command him to "stay," release the pressure, and praise him immediately. This praise helps him to relax, understand the command, and feel your approval.

As with all new exercises, you will practice this exercise for ten minutes each day until he understands and performs it without having to place him in the down position or stepping on the lead. This exercise can be very trying for some. Just keep up the exercise, and you will be surprised at the results.

The correction used for non-compliance is to raise the loop off the ground and snap the lead with your foot. Do not raise the lead so high that you have to lift your leg high in the air to place your foot in the loop. You do not want the dog to key on your leg going in the air, and you do not want so much pressure downward that you jerk his neck out of place. You want just enough pressure to make him understand that he did not do what he was supposed to do. If he still does not assume the down position, repeat the lesson, demonstrating to him what he must do.

This position places you and all others in the dominant position. This also causes some concern for your dog, as he is has placed in the most submissive position known to dogs. Be patient; he will be lying down before you know it. When you see him lie down on his own, praise him by saying, "Good boy, good down." This helps reinforce the command and the action.

In order to prevent him from becoming confused, do not always give him a sit command before giving him the down command. Give him down commands while he is standing also. If he is first made to sit before being given the down command, your dog will anticipate the down. Each time you place him in a sitting position, he will anticipate the down coming next, and instead of sitting, he will sit, and then lie down. You want him to distinguish between *sit* and *down*. In order to do this, you have to give him down commands while he is standing, as well as when he is sitting.

You should also give him sit commands from the down position. Just command him to sit, and place an upward pressure on the lead until he assumes the sitting position. This will help him learn the difference between *sit* and *down*. Do not make a snap or pop correction to have him sit. Just apply upward pressure until he rises to the sitting position.

Do not be in a rush to complete this chapter. It may take time, but you will be rewarded in the end. There is not any time limit on achieving this goal. Take your time, and continue to practice. If you feel yourself getting frustrated, stop this lesson, give a command that the dog understands and can perform without any trouble, and then end the session. Tomorrow is another day.

Chapter 25
The Stand

The stand is another exercise that is seen at dog shows. This is used so that the judge may examine the conformation structure of the dog. The dog is placed in the "stand" position, and the handler will move to the end of the lead, out of the way, and allow the judge to examine the dog without any interference. The judge will check the teeth to ensure the correct number and position of the bite; look into the dog's eyes to check the pupils and clearness of the eyes, as well as feel the skull formation and proper distance of the nose, the set and length of the ears, and the set of the shoulders and forelegs. He will pass his hand along the backbone to the croup and down the rear leg. If this is a male, he will check the testicles to be sure both have descended. In other words, the judge has given an exterior physical to your dog. This is a very valuable exercise that can be used when taking your dog to the veterinarian. When the veterinarian is ready to give your dog a shot or check him out, you simply command him to "stand/stay" while the veterinarian proceeds with his business.

This position will enable the veterinarian to accomplish his task, and you or an assistant will not have to hold the dog still. Your veterinarian will appreciate it, and you will be finished with the visit before you know it.

If you have had success with the other exercises, your dog will probably comply with this exercise without any trouble. If you have had to struggle with your dog through the previous training exercises, you may become a little frustrated with this lesson. Do not let your frustrations show if your dog begins moving toward you or sitting down after you have left him. Continue placing him into position each time he moves or sits, until he performs a stand/stay, even if it is just for ten seconds. You want him to understand what you want from him. Time can be gained after he understands the lesson.

With your dog at the heel position, turn toward him and kneel down so that he is in front of you. Move the dog's collar high on his neck so that the collar is directly behind his ears. Grasp the collar from behind his ears with your right hand, and give the command, "Stand." As you give him the command, gently pull him forward as if he were going to heel, but do not move from your position. As he begins to stand, pass your left arm under him and in front of his rear legs, assisting him into a standing position. As he stands, release the pressure on the collar, but do not release the collar. With your left arm still in position, bend your elbow and gently scratch his stomach or chest. If you scratch too hard or too fast, it will tickle the dog, and he will begin moving around out of control.

When he is standing and begins to settle down, look closely at the muscles in the rear legs and shoulders. You want to see those muscles begin to relax before you do anything else. All you are doing at this time is helping him to relax. If he is tense, he cannot learn. Tension will cause him to become anxious, and he will start moving about. He does not understand what is happening, and it is your job to help him understand.

As he begins to relax, give the command "Stay," and move directly away from him while holding his lead. Do not linger, hover over him, or spend too much time talking to him. Simply get him up with the "stand" command, and once he has relaxed, give the "stay" command, and walk to the end of your lead. Turn and face your dog.

If he understands and complies with the "stay" command, you should not have any trouble having him stay while standing. If he sits or lies down after you leave, go back to the same spot and stand him again. Continue standing and leaving him until he stays when you walk away.

When you have reached the goal of having him stand and stay, you will spend a little more time with positioning him. His front legs should be positioned under him and square with his chest. His rear legs should be out and behind him, set squarely with his rear end. The portion of his leg, from his feet to elbow, should be perpendicular to the ground.

He may resist having his legs moved around at first, but continue adjusting him until he stands in the proper position. When he is standing properly, give the command "Stay," and leave him. Stand in front of him while holding his lead.

Some dogs catch on very quickly, while others may take a few days of practice. Once you have him in the "stand-stay" position, have someone walk around him, but do not touch him at this time. If he moves, reestablish the stand. Continue this until he does not move when someone walks around him.

Next, have someone walk up to him and just touch his head, neck, back, and rear. Do not allow any petting or stroking, just gently touch him. If he moves while being touched, you must put him back in the position you left him until he allows the touching without moving. When this is accomplished, have someone touch and stroke him all over his back. If there is any movement from his feet, you must reposition him and begin again. Continue practicing this until he stands and stays during and after the person examining him has left him. Then you will return to him by circling around him and returning to the heel position.

If your dog shows signs of resistance to being touched or handled by someone other than you or your family members, he needs socialization that is more positive. Practice standing your dog in parking lots. Take him to an area where there are many people around. These distractions will help you and your dog. Once you have him standing in these distracting areas without movement, begin having someone walk around him, then advance to touching him. You want your dog to trust what you and others are doing while in your presence. Go slowly.

When at home, have your dog stand, and play with all of his feet. In fact, you should touch and play with his feet even when he is not in a formal training session. This is an area where most dogs do not want your hands. By desensitizing your dog to having his feet touched, you will have less trouble when dealing with this area.

Chapter 26
Off-lead Basics

Most owners want a dog that will obey their every command without ever having to put a lead on him. The problem that most owners encounter is a dog that runs off and does whatever he wants, while the owner stands frustrated, calling for the dog to return to him. Hurling obscenities and making threats of what will happen to him if he does not listen are usually in the scenario.

Here is the solution to this problem: Do not remove the lead from your dog until he understands everything he must do while he is on lead and does it without hesitation or correction every time he is given a command. Do not test your dog to see if he will listen. Once he realizes that you do not have any control over him and cannot correct him, he has won the battle of wills for freedom, and you have to start over with training, after you catch him. If this type of training continues, the dog will do everything he can to stay out of your reach, to prevent you from putting him on the lead. There is a time for testing, but not until he understands and responds every time. Do not be in a rush to get through the training.

Owners will work with their dogs on lead and are very pleased with the way the dog reacts to his training. They remove the lead, expecting the dog to respond in the same manner, and the dog goes about his business as if the owners were not there. All the screaming and yelling in the world will not get him back to you. Do not test your dog until he understands and performs each task without error, unless you like continuous, never-ending training combined with running after your dog.

Off-lead work takes a little time, but it can be achieved. When the dog has completed all of his on-lead work, understands the commands and responds to those commands without fail, then you can begin doing off-lead work. A training tab is required during this training.

A training tab is a short strap about three inches long. They may be purchased through pet stores and catalogs. It can be fashioned by using a short section of line and a snap, which may be purchased from the local hardware store. Place the tab on his collar while you work with him on lead. Corrections for any mistakes or non-compliance will be made using the tab, and not the lead. This lets the dog know that you can still correct him, even though it did not come from the lead, and will get his attention.

You will also need a light line. This may be purchased at the local hardware store. Explain to the salesman that you want pull cord for a chainsaw. You will need approximately twenty-five feet. While there, purchase a bull snap, one that is large enough to fit the dog's collar.

Begin by attaching the training tab and a light line to the training collar. Allow approximately three inches of slack hanging from the dog's collar, and tie the other end of the line around your waist. Place the remainder of the cord in your pocket after tying it around your waist. Place your arms in front of you at waist level. Now you are ready to begin.

Start with a simple heeling exercise. Command your dog to heel and begin moving in the same manner as you would if you were using

The Abney Method to Owning a Dog

the lead. If he hesitates, the line will pull him into action. If he resists in any way, grab the training tab and pull him forward as you would with the regular training lead. You do not want to handle the line unless it becomes necessary. Continue practicing the simple heeling exercise until he understands that he must obey without any corrections.

Once the heeling is going well, begin doing turns. This can be a bit tricky, especially the left turn, but if he was working well on lead, there should not be a problem with this exercise. Continue doing the heeling and turning exercises for about one week.

After the weeklong training, if he is doing well, you will begin practicing the "slip lead" technique. With the tab in place, double your lead in half and place one end under his collar and hold both ends in your hand. Begin heeling and stopping. When you make one of the stops, gently slide the line so that one end is just under his collar. As you begin the heel, allow the line to slip out from under his collar. Do not hesitate or make a fuss about it; simply slide the line out as you are heeling. Continue heeling and stopping without the line attached. If there is any hesitation, make your correction using the tab. If he refuses to cooperate, return to using the slip-lead method. Continue until he understands that you can still correct him even if he has no lead on him.

Once he is heeling and turning without corrections, begin training the drop-in-motion. Remember to keep his tab in place during training at all times. While you are heeling your dog, have him go into the down position. Give a down-stay command, and continue walking without the dog for approximately fifteen feet. Do not stop when you give the command, but hesitate long enough for him to understand that he must go down. Give the command as if it were one command and not two. Say "Down-stay," and continue walking with as little interruption to your movement as possible. It must be as fluid as possible. When you reach your distance, turn and face your dog. Wait for about twenty to twenty-five seconds and call your dog to you. When he comes, be sure that he performs the sit in front. If he attempts to run past you, grab the tab and make him do a sit in front. If he begins to run past you and out of reach, then you should attach his training lead to his collar and perform the exercise with the lead attached. Simply drop the lead on the ground when you give the down-stay command. The lead will slow him down when he comes, and if he runs past you, just step on the lead to stop him. After a few of these, use the slip line by placing him in the down-stay and slipping the lead out from his collar as you walk away. When you call your dog and he comes to you, make him sit in front and do the finish as you would if he were on lead.

It is best to "proof" the dog in an enclosed area first. Then, if an error occurs, you will be able to retrieve your dog without too much chasing around or endangering it. If you have to chase the dog around, he will lose focus on the lesson, and you will have to begin again. When he complies with the heel and down-in-motion while only on his training tab, end the lesson. Success is the key. If you were successful, you only have to build confidence in the dog and your ability to control the situation.

If your dog is one that is fully aware of when the lead or line is attached to him, try using a length of nylon fishing line attached to his collar. This line is light enough that it cannot be felt by the dog, yet strong enough to make minor corrections, and it will remind him that you still have control. Work with the dog in the same manner you would if you were using a lead, but use the line instead. You must be careful when using fishing line. The line is thin and strong, and it can cause a bad cut to your hands. It is best to tie the line to your belt to avoid any damage to your hands.

Now that your dog understands the heel, turns, stay, come, finish, and drop-in-motion, you may proceed to teaching the drop-on-recall. Place your dog in the down-stay and walk approximately fifty feet away from him. Facing your dog, call him to you. When he is about halfway to you, command him to "Down." As you command down, extend your arms in front of you and move one arm straight up and the other straight down as you give the command. If the dog does not go down, step toward him, place him in the down, and walk back to your position. Allow him to remain in the down for about thirty seconds and then call him. Do the sit in front and finish. Continue performing this exercise until he will drop when you command him. This exercise is used in obedience shows, but I find it useful for owners who like to take their dogs to parks. If there is any problem, you know you can down your dog from a distance. This comes in handy when your dog attempts to cross a street in traffic. You can down him until it is safe for him to come to you.

Be patient. Some dogs catch on very quickly, but for others it takes a little time for the dog to understand exactly what it is you want from him. Try to keep this in mind. When you were a child and taken to a park, the first thing you did when you were not being controlled by your parent was to run around, throw yourself on the ground, and turn a deaf ear to that yelling adult. Your dog is no different. It is time to play, and the world is open to him. Take your time, and be patient. Everything must be learned, and each thing takes time. Be consistent with your praise and corrections. Be sure the dog understands any exercise prior to giving any praise or making any correction. Be certain that the dog is completely reliable on one exercise prior to moving on to another. Remember: patience, timing, consistency, and motivation. These are the elements required for proper training.

Chapter 27
What Next?

O kay, you've trained your dog to do all those things in the book, and now you are wondering what you will do next. Well, your training hasn't ended. Just because the dog learned the exercises doesn't mean that he won't forget them. He must be reminded, a minimum of once each week. Take him out for a walk and put him through his paces. Repetition will help him to remember. When you were learning to add fractions in school, it would sometimes be difficult. You succeeded because you continued to work at it, and you learned what sequence must be done in order to be successful. If you don't continue working with those fractions on occasion, you will forget those lessons. The same holds true for your dog. If he is not reminded of the lessons and exercises, he will lapse into doing only the ones he wants to perform.

How will you train him for other things? Perhaps you've decided that you want to compete with your dog in obedience trials, flyball, or Frisbee events.

If that's what you want to do, then proceed with training your dog to compete. The training for basic obedience, novice classes, features the same lessons listed in this book. You will have to fine tune your dog for him to perform to the best of his ability and for him to respond immediately to each command or hand signal.

The rules for obedience trials vary from one organization to another, so you will have to learn the rules and what is expected of the dog by each organization before you enter their competitions. The basic obedience trials will include heeling and figure eights, both on and off lead, recall (come), stand for examination, long sit (one minute) and long down (three minutes).

Once you have completed this portion, you may advance to higher levels of obedience and tracking. Since this book is intended for the everyday dog owner, I will not go into all the requirements that must be completed. There are many books on the subject, and I would strongly suggest that you work with a professional trainer.

Training is not hard. It is sometimes trying, but not hard. You already have the basics for what needs to be done. Just apply those basic skills toward the next thing you want your dog to do.

Complex actions using a simple command must be broken down into simple actions first. Each action must be accomplished before you can go to the next part of the sequence. For example, you would like your dog to fetch your newspaper. This can be accomplished by giving the dog a simple word such as "paper" to have him run out the door, find the paper, pick it up, carry it back to you, and drop it at your feet. In order for him to fetch the paper, there are a few other things he must learn. He must be taught to hold the paper in his mouth and not destroy it. He must be taught to let it go. He must be taught to retrieve it from a particular location. He must be taught to bring the paper back to where you are. It's a simple command requiring a variety of actions. Just break down the action that you wish and start training the basics of each sequence before you try to accomplish it in its entire sequence.

I had a friend who would have his dog fetch his gloves and hammer for him. People were amazed that the dog would continue to fetch the articles asked for each time his owner asked him. What they didn't know was that the dog had been trained to fetch in a certain order. Everything had to be laid out properly for it to work. He would lay his gloves on a table with the left glove first, the right glove next to it, and the hammer next. When he would send the dog to retrieve, he would say, "Fetch my left glove," and the dog would run off, get the first glove (left) and bring it back. He would then repeat the sequence for the other glove and hammer. People would talk about how smart this dog was because he knew the difference between the left and right glove and could identify the hammer.

Was it just a trick? To some degree it was, but the dog had to be taught the retrieve sequence before any of the fun could begin. Every now and then during training, the dog would bring the wrong glove. Was he making a mistake or showing his owner he could have fun too?

Training should be broken down into simple actions. Train the simple actions first, and combine those simple actions into one command, creating a complex action.

Work with your dog. It only takes fifteen minutes each day to teach him. The biggest problem most people have is accepting what the dog is giving them. If you work with your dog for fifteen minutes and he performs well, stop working. Accept what he has done. You and he have been successful. Why continue on and create frustration for yourself and your dog? He does not have to repeat the action twenty times, or even three times in succession. Once is enough. Tomorrow is another day for more success. If you overwork your dog, it will only lead to failure.

Chapter 28
Problem-solving

Dog owners are capable of solving the majority of problems in dogs, because the dog owner creates most of the problems unknowingly. One of the biggest ones is that the owner plays with the puppy when it first comes into the home, but as time goes on and the puppy begins to grow into an adult, that same playtime becomes very limited. Then there is a problem. The dog becomes bored and looks for things to occupy it. Unfortunately, the things that the dog finds enjoyable are not what make us happy. I have listed some of the most common problems that owners have with their pets, and the solutions I find to be most effective. There are many books written on dogs and their problems, but again I believe that the owners create most problems. If you have tried to solve a problem unsuccessfully, seek a professional trainer who can work with you and your dog. I would also refer you to a book entitled *Behavior Problems in Dogs* written by William E. Campbell. Mr. Campbell's approach to problems, causes, and cures are of great value to anyone owning a dog and wanting to solve or avoid some serious problems.

For the most part, if you have done any training with your dog, you will be on the path to eliminating most of the common annoyance problems people have with their dogs. Obedience training presents the dog with a job. If he has a job to do, his mind is busy. He is listening to your commands and waiting for the next one. Boredom is a dog's worst enemy and an owner's nightmare.

Most of the problems discussed in the Puppy chapter can be applied to your adult dog. The one thing to keep in mind is that you are dealing with a mature dog. Thinking that raising your voice and throwing him around are going to make him understand or behave any better are wrong. As I was told in my early years as a trainer, "If you want to train a dog, you have to be smarter than the dog." This may sound like sarcasm, but it is the truth. Dogs will try to outsmart you if you allow them. You must be in control and always thinking ahead of the dog's next action or his response to your actions. Like a Boy Scout, you must "be prepared."

Housetraining

Many housetraining problems stem from owners who start out by placing newspaper on the floor and directing their dog to eliminate on the paper. Unless you want to train your dog to eliminate in your home, do not put newspapers on the floor and direct him to use them. You are teaching your dog that it is okay to relieve himself in the house. This is not what you really want, so do not give any indication that it is okay to eliminate in the house. Placing paper on the floor may make it faster and easier to remove his waste from the home, but it will only serve to confuse the dog when you decide that he needs to eliminate outdoors. If you want him to eliminate outdoors, then start outdoors.

As you begin housetraining, you must be aware of the times your dog—and especially a young puppy—is eating. Puppies do not hold their food for very long, and will usually relieve themselves within ten to fifteen minutes of eating. If you are leaving food available for your puppy to eat whenever he wants, commonly referred to as *free choice,* then you will encounter some problems training your dog. If you are not aware of when he is eating, then you will not know when he needs to relieve himself.

"If you control the food, you control the dog"

From birth until the first solid food was presented to the puppies, feeding time was dependent on the puppy's mother. If she did not want to lie down and nurse them, then they had to wait for her. When she felt it was time for them to eat, she would feed them. Food was not available to them around the clock, but regulated. The reason for this regulation was to give them time to digest their food. A young puppy's stomach is extremely small and cannot hold a great amount of food, and since they are on a liquid diet, digestion is rapid. Young puppies cannot relieve themselves and must be stimulated to do so. While nursing, or directly after nursing, she licks each of the pups, stimulating them to relieve themselves. This ritual of eating and relieving is a learned response that lingers with the pups long after weaning. Puppies will eat, play, or exercise, then look for a place to relieve themselves shortly after eating, until such time as they are capable of holding their bowel and bladder functions for a longer period.

A puppy will require being fed two to three times a day. At feeding time, allow the puppy fifteen to twenty minutes to eat and drink as much as it desires, then pick up the food. If the puppy has played through its feeding time, then so be it. Pick up the food and offer it at the next feeding time. You should not give your puppy any other food or treats while you are housetraining. When the next feeding time comes, he will concentrate on getting something to eat. If he does not eat, do not become overly concerned. By the third feeding, he will be more than happy to eat. This is controlling the food. As you continue along with this program, you will see how it helps to control the dog.

Ensure that fresh water is always available to him, even if he skips eating. A dog can miss a few meals, but he cannot exist without water. Be certain that your dog is drinking, even if you have to take him to the bowl to get a drink.

After your puppy has finished eating and/or drinking, give the verbal command "Outside," and take him outside. Remain outside with the puppy until he has completed both functions. This may take ten to twenty minutes for a puppy, and as much as forty-five minutes for a larger dog. *Do not* leave him alone or engage in any play activity with him until he has relieved himself. Simply sit outside with him and wait for him to relieve himself. Placing him outdoors by himself and expecting him to do what you want is wishful thinking at best. Putting him out alone is going to create a feeling of abandonment, and he will not concentrate on relieving himself, but will utilize all his efforts in regaining access to your presence.

When he finds a spot and begins to eliminate, give a verbal command such as "Hurry up," "Go potty," or "Take a break" while he is eliminating. As soon as he is finished, you must praise him verbally and physically. You cannot stand in a corner and tell him he did well. You have to go to him and apply praise. Pat, stroke, and tell him what a good puppy he is, while repeating the command. For example, pet him and say, "Good boy, good hurry up." Hearing your voice of pleasure and being touched will help teach him what you want him to do. He is learning that it pleases you when he goes outside to do his business. Using the command words during the elimination period will teach your dog to go on your command. You will appreciate this command and its response on those rainy days or when you are in a hurry.

Now that the elimination process is completed, allow the puppy time to play and explore for an additional ten to fifteen minutes. Do not pick him up and take him inside immediately after he has finished eliminating. Taking the puppy inside immediately after elimination will serve to discourage him going out to eliminate, because he has no time to play. Then, when he is placed outside, he will begin to hold his bowel movements so that he has time to play while outside, and then eliminate when he is taken back inside. Give the pup some time to play when he has finished eliminating. This will assure him that he is allowed to play, and that being outside to eliminate is not a punishment. When he has expended some of his pent-up energy, take him inside. Most puppies and dogs learn this exercise in seven to ten days. Be patient and do not try to rush him.

If you have a particular spot in your yard where you would like your pup to go to relieve himself, then try the following: Purchase a bottle of sudsy household ammonia and pour it in the area you desire. Allow it to seep into the soil, and then expose him to that area. The dog will be attracted to the smell of the ammonia—believing that another dog has used that area—and will begin using it as his own.

Accidents in the House

If your puppy has an accident in the house, do not rub his nose in it or spank him. I could never figure out what was accomplished by rubbing a dog's nose in its mess. He knows what it is, and he already knows how it smells, so what are you telling this dog? Absolutely nothing! You are only confusing the dog with this type of action, and the dog will learn to hide his mess behind the furniture so that you cannot see it. Should you find an area where he has already eliminated in your house, simply give the command "Outside" in a calm voice, place him in his yard, and then clean up the mess. **Do not** allow the puppy to watch you cleaning up his mess. If he is allowed to watch you, he will think you liked it and soon do it again.

Clean up the mess with a non-ammonia-based product. Ammonia is in urine and feces, and the pup will think that another dog was there and marked the same spot where he eliminated. He will be attracted back to that spot, and attempt to place his mark where that "other" dog marked his territory.

If you catch your puppy in the act, you should calmly say "Outside," pick him up, and take him out. Keep in mind that you interrupted him, and it may take a little longer for him to get going again.

Do not yell at him. Yelling at him while he is eliminating could cause him to think that he must not let you see him eliminate, and he will begin hiding to relieve himself so that he is not reprimanded. This problem can be harder to correct than simple housetraining.

Be consistent with this training, and you will be rewarded with a dog that eliminates outdoors within seven to ten days.

Crate Training

The shipping- and holding-type containers used for transporting dogs via airlines are referred to as crates. They may be made of wire, plastic, or a combination of the two. The crate should be of a size that will allow the dog ease of movement when inside. Ideally, there should be enough room in the crate for the dog to stand comfortably and turn around. The size can be determined by measuring your dog from the ground to the withers (top of shoulder), then adding four inches.

Some owners believe the use of crates in the home is cruel and uncaring. So that there is no misunderstanding about the use of crates, let us look at what dogs in the wild do.

Dogs are territorial and mark their surroundings with their scent by urinating on the ground or objects in the area that they have claimed as theirs. This tells other dogs that may wander into this area that this territory has been claimed. Within the territory, a dog will seek out a small, enclosed area, called a den. The den is the dog's safe haven, where it will sleep and go to escape danger or bad weather. The den is generally a place that is completely covered, except for the entrance, and resembles a cave. This offers the dog a means of feeling safe from any attacks from the rear, where he has only to watch the opening for oncoming danger. This allows the dog the opportunity to escape or defend his domain. He is comfortable knowing that he has to guard only one opening, and that nothing can approach from any other direction. This instinct is in all dogs: wild and domestic. Crate training is a means of providing your dog his own place of safety, his den, within the home.

Why crate train? It provides the dog with a place of his own, where he can feel secure and comfortable. It provides the owner with a means of removing the dog from the presence of those who are uncomfortable around dogs, without completely isolating the dog from its family.

It is best to start crate training your dog while he is still a puppy. This will help establish some of the ground rules, without causing too much stress. Start by placing a toy or treat in the crate and letting him go inside to get it. Allow him to go slowly. A new crate has a number of different scents on it, and it may be a bit confusing to him. Before you acquired the crate, numerous people handled it, and their scents are on it as well. Just let the puppy take his time. Do not force the puppy into the crate, as this will scare him and cause him to develop a fear of being placed in it. If this happens, you will have to fight with him just to get him inside. This also applies to a used crate. If you acquire a crate that was used by another dog, your dog will be reluctant to go inside. It's best to clean the crate thoroughly with bleach prior to using it. Be sure to rinse it thoroughly. Any bleach left behind can cause an irritation to the dog's skin.

Once the puppy is in the crate, play with him. Do not close the door. Block the opening with your body, but allow him the time to become comfortable in knowing that the crate is not a danger. When he is going in and out of the crate freely and without hesitation, you may then close the door.

When the door is closed and the puppy realizes that he cannot get out, he may begin to chew or claw the crate, or he may begin howling or barking. If this happens, ignore him. Any attention you pay him while he is trying to escape the crate tells the dog that he can get your attention by chewing, clawing, barking, or howling. The dog is now training you. Allow him some time to settle down and relax. Remember to leave a toy with him, to prevent him from being bored. Once he has calmed down and rested for approximately twenty minutes, you may allow him out of his crate. Do not release him from the crate while he is misbehaving. This will only serve to tell him that the more noise and fuss he creates, the more attention he will get.

This training will require a few days of this ritual, until the pup realizes that he must go in the crate and remain quiet if he wants to be allowed out. When placing him in the crate, use a command word such as "Crate" or "Kennel" to help instill in him the action you want.

Choose a word, and stick with it. Changing the command word, or mixing it with other commands, will only confuse the dog.

The majority of crating problems arise when dogs are placed in open wire crates for them to spend the night. The dog will become anxious, because he has to watch all sides of an open wire crate for signs of danger. You will find that covering the crate with a sheet or some type of cover, so that only the door may be viewed, will eliminate the stress and help to get the dog inside.

When training a dog that is past the puppy stage, it can be a bit trying. If the dog is not used to a crate and struggles with you when placing him in his crate, try placing him in the crate backward. In other words, position him so that his rear goes into the crate first. By easing him backward into the crate, he is always looking at you and will feel more at ease. Your hands will be all over him, he can see you, and he will feel safe.

Crate training will help minimize separation anxiety and avoid destructive behavior.

A dog that is allowed full run of the house, especially when no one is there, will eventually become bored, and find something with which to entertain himself, and it usually is not the type of entertainment that pleases the owner. After all, staying home alone can be boring, and rearranging furniture, woodwork, carpet, and clothing can be a lot more fun than just lying on the floor, waiting for someone to come home and play.

Separation Anxiety

A great many separation anxiety problems begin at the puppy stage and advance throughout the adolescent years and into adulthood. Owners think they are doing what is right, but they are actually creating this problem.

A lot of time is spent with the puppy while it is new. This is good for the puppy's socialization, but he becomes dependent on the pack. There must be a balance of socialization and isolation, or independence. By spending too much time with the puppy, you are conveying to him that he does not have to worry about anything, because the pack is strong and someone is always there to take care of him. This can cause the puppy to become dependent on those around him and lose his assertiveness.

As the puppy begins to grow, less time is spent playing with him, and the training sessions become shorter and further apart. The pack always goes away to work, school, etc., and the puppy is left behind. Not only is he left behind, the pack goes through this ritual of letting him know he is being left by giving him hugs, kisses, and pats of reassurance that you will return. You believe he should be reassured, but what your dog hears is, "I'm leaving, and you can't come with me. Ha, ha, ha!" The puppy gets the feeling of being abandoned. He becomes anxious at your leaving, and he begins to bark, howl, run in circles, and eventually tries to grab hold of your clothing or your hand so you cannot leave. You stop what you are doing and try to console the dog. You think you are reassuring him about your leaving and returning, but all the dog knows is that he is going to be left alone.

Your dog is not able to be with you, and he is not in a place that he considers his den. As he advances toward adulthood, these reassurances become more and more commonplace, and the anxiety builds in the dog. He becomes more anxious about your leaving, and totally out of control when you return. Here is what is happening inside the dog.

You have said your goodbyes and he is now alone. All the barking, howling, and carrying on, running up and down inside the house have not brought you back, so the dog settles on the next best thing to your being there—your scent. Your scent is all over the house, and if the dog has full run of the house, he is going to seek it out. He will find the places where the scent is the strongest, such as shoes, clothes, sofa, bedding, etc., and his wanting to have your company will bring him to destructive behavior. This is *separation anxiety*.

He becomes anxious with your coming and going, along with the attention he receives at each of these periods, which reinforces the fact that he is being left behind. He may begin by running up and down the house, barking incessantly, or howling while you are gone. When that does not bring you back, the destructive behavior begins by chewing personal belongings, woodwork, furniture, etc.

To help eliminate separation anxiety, you must utilize crate training. Begin by placing your dog in a crate for short periods while you are home. He may make a ruckus at being placed in the crate, but ignore him. Let him bark or howl, but do not talk to him until he settles down for at least fifteen minutes. When he has quieted down and is calm for fifteen to twenty minutes, allow him out of his crate. Wait approximately four hours and repeat the process. This method will have him become accustomed to being in the crate while you are home, and will help him to accept the fact that he must be in the crate (his new den) while you are away.

After he adjusts to being in the crate, place him in his crate using the above method, fifteen to twenty minutes prior to leaving, and then just go out of the house for about ten minutes and come back inside. Wait about five minutes prior to talking to the dog. Repeat this daily and extend the time you are gone. This will help to calm him, giving him the positive reassurance that you are going to return. In time, the barking and howling while you are gone will end.

When you have to leave him alone for a longer period, place him in his crate fifteen minutes prior to your leaving. Be calm with him, pet and talk to him at the time you place him in the crate, and then do whatever duties you must perform before leaving the house. When it is time for you to go, leave without saying a word to the dog. DO NOT TALK TO THE DOG! Just go about your business of leaving as if he were not there.

When you arrive home, DO NOT immediately tend to the dog. He has been waiting all day for you to come home, and now that you are there, you should not make him the most important thing for your attention upon entering. Instead of visiting with him, go to the bathroom, take out the trash, or do something that will take about fifteen to twenty minutes of your time. He knows you are there, he can smell you, but he has not yet been paid a visit. After the elapsed time of fifteen to twenty minutes, allow him out of the crate.

If he becomes out of control or overly excited, place him in a sit-stay and make him wait to be petted. He will begin to understand that the pack has things it must do before attention is given to him. You place a structure in the dog's life that he will understand, and his confidence will be restored. The pack is there, but it has other things it must do. The pack is not there just for his entertainment.

When crating, you should leave something that will keep him occupied. One way is to give him his favorite toy. One method I like to use is to place some creamy peanut butter inside a Kong toy. He will spend hours trying to get the peanut butter out, and he will not become anxious while the pack is gone. Another idea is to place a treat inside a hollow, bone-shaped toy.

Chewing

Chewing, or "Boy, this feels good on my gums," can drive owners to insanity. Insanity? Oh, yes. I have had clients say that if I did not find a way to stop this chewing, they would positively go insane. I have never seen anyone actually go insane from puppy chewing, but I have met some very anxious clients. The problem of chewing is generally not the puppy's fault. He does not have hands, so investigating anything is generally done with the mouth. In addition, he is trying to get relief from those annoying teeth that are growing in his mouth. What happens is that the owner thinks they are doing a good thing by giving the puppy an old shoe or sock to chew on. It keeps the puppy quiet, and that suits the owner. Unfortunately, the puppy knows only scent and not adjectives. If you gave him an *old* shoe to chew on, do not get angry when he chews up your *good* shoes. Those "good" shoes have the same scent as the old ones. Socks? They have your scent on them, and they are fabric. Your scent is everywhere. You told him it was okay to chew these things, and now he is. The best way to avoid chewing problems is to keep them from starting. Tug-of-war games are the common cause of chewing. The best thing you can do is to get your dog a nylon bone—beef or chicken flavored are best—or a hard rubber toy. Some of the hard rubber toys have a hole in them where

223

you can place a little peanut butter inside. This will keep your puppy busy for hours, and his chewing will be directed where it cannot cause any harm.

Puppies will chew to ease the discomfort of teeth breaking through the gums. Chewing is the only way a puppy can get relief from this irritation. Give the puppy something that is safe for him to chew on. If he ventures into another area or object, correct him by removing him from the area or object, and give him his toy. If he insists on going back to the object, grab the scruff of his neck, give a short shake, and give him his toy. This action is okay with a puppy, but be careful about shaking an older dog. Removal of an older dog may have to be by lead, but do remove him.

Keep in mind that a puppy's teeth will undergo more changes at ten months of age. Most people do not realize this and confuse it with a behavior problem. They believe the dog has become spiteful. This is not the case. At approximately ten months of age, the dog will go through some other oral changes, and the chewing will begin again. Just be ready for it.

Each puppy should be given no more than two toys to play with. One of the toys should be a hard, plastic, bone-shaped, flavored toy. Pet stores carry such products, which I have found work extremely well. I have had good success with the beef- and chicken-flavored bones. I have also had success with a Kong toy. I discourage using rawhide, pig ears, cow hooves, and the like, because the puppy will obtain a level of success in destroying these things. In addition to the destruction factor, it gets to ingest the object. What does all this mean? It means that he has won a victory over the opponent, and he must move on to another opponent. That next opponent may be your furniture, woodwork, or something he considers a challenge.

If you catch your dog in the act of chewing, correct him by saying, "Leave it," and distract him with his own chew toy. If your puppy is insistent on getting back to the other article, move either the puppy or the article. You must be persistent in your instructions and consistent in your training. If he moves back ten times, make the correction eleven times. Do not let the puppy win.

There are "no-chew" or "stop-chew" products on the market that are supposed to stop your dog from chewing. Some people have had success with them, and others have not. I have had people use hot sauce on articles to deter the chewing, only to have their dogs develop a taste for hot sauce. The only tried-and-true methods are persistence and consistency.

I had a dog that loved to chew up her stainless steel food bowl. She had also destroyed four metal buckets. What was my solution? I placed her water bucket inside a larger bucket, and tied it down so that it could not be moved. Her food bowl was chained to her pen so it could not be taken off, and I gave her a hard plastic dumbbell to play with. Did she stop chewing the bucket? No! She did not pay as much attention to them as she once did, but she would occasionally attack the bowl and bucket. Since they could not be moved, she would give up rapidly, saving the bowl and bucket from destruction. I believe that she just got bored, which is generally the case with destructive chewing. My reason for tying down her bowl and bucket was to save her teeth. She had chipped several teeth by chewing on these objects. With some dogs, you have to be inventive. She was a good dog, very obedient, but she liked the sound of that bowl and bucket hitting the pavement, and she enjoyed the attack. Occupy your dog's attention with its own toys. This discourages destructive chewing and allows it to get lots of exercise.

Mouthing and Biting

When I receive calls concerning a puppy that is biting or mouthing, the first question I ask is, "Are you playing tug of war with your puppy? Are there any roughhouse games?" In most cases, the answer is yes. Although a game of tug of war seems harmless enough, you are strengthening the biting power and the jaw muscles of your puppy. After tugging for a while, you probably get tired of the game and let the puppy have the object. Now you have taught the puppy that it can win by biting and being persistent. Playing tug of war creates more problems in dogs than any other game. The technique used in tug-of-war games is the same as that used for training an attack dog. Unless you desire your dog to bite or mouth you, stop playing tug of war.

Another thing that I hear when I am giving instructions about mouthing is, "Oh, he's only playing; he doesn't really mean to hurt." Wrong! He is testing to see what amount of power must be used to win this game and how far he has to go before you are hurt. Then, when he hurts you, you slap him on the side of his face or on top of his nose. This is not going to stop him or teach him not to continue. This is another technique used to incite an attack dog. Stop slapping the dog.

Why do some people think it is fun to roll a puppy on his back, place their hand on his stomach, and shake him until he is growling and trying to bite? This is not a game to the puppy. This is a challenge for position of authority. Puppies will do this very thing in the litter in order to establish the pecking order. Face-biting, mouthing, and pinning is a part of a game that helps to establish where in the pecking order a puppy will belong. When you place your pup on his back and taunt him, you are challenging him. Continuously doing this will only have your puppy resenting you and this game.

If you watch a litter closely, you will see this game take place. When one of the puppies attempts to establish its dominance over the other, a small fight breaks out. It does not last very long, and each puppy goes in a different direction when it is over. The winner or dominant dog always walks away first. Everyone thinks this is cute and laughs at the little puppies pretending to be grown dogs. What you have witnessed is two puppies attempting to establish their rank, or pecking order, within the pack. When your puppy is mouthing or biting at you, he is attempting to declare his dominance over you.

The correction that I find most effective is the under-jaw correction, or uppercut. When done correctly, the puppy is surprised and confused by the action. First, make a fist with your palm up. Next, move your thumb to the side of your hand. With the knuckles exposed, quickly move your hand upward, in an uppercut fashion, to make the puppy's mouth close quickly. When done properly, this action will cause the teeth to clash together. Your puppy will not like the sensation of his teeth clashing, and he will quickly move away. Once distracted from the mouthing, give him a toy that he can chew on, and continue playing using the toy.

A few of these corrections will generally stop the mouthing and biting. If you should make a correction, and your puppy growls or charges you, grab him by the nape of the neck and roll him to the floor on his back. Place your hand on his stomach and hold him there until he stops struggling. Do not let him up until he stops struggling. This maneuver is referred to as the "alpha roll," and can be effective when used on a puppy. DO NOT attempt the alpha roll on an adult dog. The results could be disastrous for you. An adult dog could view this as a challenge and not a correction. Because of his maturity, he would fight harder to get up, and would attempt to bite the person holding him down. If he is successful in having you allow him to get up, your problems have doubled. He will believe he has power over you, and will begin challenging you in other areas.

If your puppy starts to lick your hand after a correction has been made, praise him and allow the licking, as long as it does not escalate to mouthing or biting again. Any further attempt to place your hand in his mouth should be met with another immediate correction.

The technique may be used on an adult dog, but there is a variation. The dog will be placed in a down position either prone or on its side. You must be on top of him in an instant, and you will have to hold his head firmly in place. Picture this: The dog will be lying on its side, you will be lying over him with his feet away from you, and your arm will be holding his head to the floor. You will have to hold this position until the dog stops struggling. When he stops, hold the position for approximately fifteen additional seconds, and then let him up. As you let him up from the down position, walk quietly away. Say nothing to the dog. This technique is the same one utilized by the wolf pack to assert dominance over the pack.

An adult dog is stronger, faster, and much more persistent than a puppy. He will use whatever tactics he can to survive this attack from you. An adult dog perceives this action as an attack, so if you feel that you cannot handle the above procedure, let a professional handle any biting or aggression involving an adult dog. They have the experience and ability to handle these types of dogs.

Begging

This problem is definitely owner-created. A dog will look at the owner longingly or quizzically, and the owner thinks this is so cute, it must be rewarded. Great! You are now on your way to training a beggar. Just because your dog looks at you or stares when you are eating does not mean that he should be rewarded. Do not feed the dog from the table. In fact, do not feed the dog table food. If you feel that you must give him a treat because he has been the most wonderful dog in the world, make him earn it. Have him perform a sit, down, stand, roll over, or something else to earn the treat.

If he insists on sitting and looking up at you at mealtimes or is getting into your lap to see what you have, it is time to remove the dog. Place him either outside or in his crate during mealtimes. Oh yes, and stop the kids from sneaking him food. Dogs know who their pals are when it comes to food, and they will go to the kids every time.

In the instances where this condition has already been formed, it is going to take some time to resolve. Begin by placing the dog in a down-stay as you eat. If he refuses to stay down, then you must work on that part of his training until he understands that once placed in a down, he cannot move until released. I have seen dogs hold a three-hour down-stay. It can be accomplished, but it takes work.

To begin retraining your dog to stop begging, you will have to curtail all treats you have been giving him for no reason. If he deserves a treat, give him one, but he must perform some feat before getting it. A sit or down, as previously mentioned, will help him to understand that he will get the treat only after he obeys the command. In this manner, you're conditioning him to wait until you are satisfied with his performance prior to giving him the treat. He will begin holding the stays until you release and reward him. This will stop the begging.

Carsickness

Some puppies will get carsick the first time they ride. Others will get sick every time they ride. It is a new motion, being experienced without having to move their feet. It happens to people, so do not get upset with your dog. All that is happening is his stomach gets upset.

The first sign of carsickness—actually motion sickness—is the lack of animation in your dog. Next comes drooling. You will see your pup begin to drool profusely. If the ride is a long one, the pup will usually empty his stomach and continue to drool.

There are dogs that never get carsick. Some are able to build a tolerance to the motion of the car, but it takes time. If the only time your dog gets to ride is when he goes to the vet, one of two things is going to happen: First, he knows that every time he gets in the car, he ends up at the veterinarian's office, where he is poked and prodded, and usually ends up with a shot, and that is not what he considers a fun outing. He will fight to keep from getting in the car, because the only time he gets in the car, he is headed for the veterinarian. Second, he is not used to the motion of the car, and it is going to affect his equilibrium and his stomach, making him throw up. Pretty simple!

The training required here is going to take time, so do not expect this to be done in a few days. Place the dog in the car, and allow him to just sit or walk around for a while. After about ten minutes, take him out of the car, and that part of training is over for the day. If you want to do this twice a day, make certain there is a three- to four-hour break between sessions. Continue placing him in the car until he is getting in willingly and no longer fighting you.

Once he has accepted the fact that the car is not a danger, take him for a short drive. Travel about three or four blocks and stop. In the time it takes to travel four blocks, the dog may begin to feel the symptoms of being sick, but he will not throw up.

After stopping, take him out of the car and walk around with him for about ten minutes. After he has relaxed, put him back into the car and drive home. When you get home, take him out of the car, praise him for being such a great dog, and let him play for another ten minutes before you attempt any other training. Continue doing this for about three days, and then increase your distance by one or two blocks. Again, spend two to three days working at this distance and then advance. Within a few weeks, you will be able to travel all over town, your dog will not get sick, and you will not have to worry about cleaning up the car.

Taking the short rides will also help the dog relax, and those vet visits will not be so hard. When he is traveling well, start taking a few trips to the vet's office just to say hello, not for any examination or shots, just a visit. If the vet is not too busy, ask if he will come out and pet the dog, just to say hello. This will help to relax him and relieve some of the stress about being there.

Now let us put this in perspective. If the only time you were to get a ride was when you had to go to the doctor, I bet you would put up a fight when they tried to get you into the car. Therefore, you see, those short rides let the dog know that he will not be going to the vet each time he gets into the car, and the visits to the vet will not always be so stressful.

If the dog is one that does not show any improvement, try giving him about one teaspoonful of liquid antacid approximately fifteen minutes prior to traveling, in order to help settle his stomach. This helps some dogs get over the problem. Prescription medications are available for this problem, and Dramamine administered by body weight may ease the situation. There is a side effect to doing this: The dog will become drowsy and listless for approximately eight to ten hours. I do not suggest doing this without checking with your veterinarian and ensuring that your dog can handle the medication.

Do not expect any training to work after the first or second try. It takes a little longer for some dogs to adjust. Some have taken up to eight weeks. Be patient and consistent, and it will happen.

Chasing

If you are having trouble with your puppy chasing children, the solution is simple. Have the children stop running, or remove the puppy from the area. A puppy will chase after anything that moves. Feet are one of the things puppies like to attack most, because they are low to the ground, within his field of vision, and easy to get. If they are moving, even more fun.

Chase is a dog's favorite game. They will chase after balls, string, towels, sticks, and anything that gets their attention. Movement is the key. If the movement stops, the game is over.

In most cases, the reason the children are running away is that the puppy is biting them. If the movement is stopped, the puppy stops chasing. Then you can make the correction required to stop the biting. The biggest problem people have is making the children understand. The children just want that ball of fluff with all those pointed teeth to stop biting. You have to be there to supervise the event. Once the chase stops, the correction for biting is enforced. Once the biting stops, the game becomes more fun for both the children and the puppy. The children do not have to worry about the puppy biting them, and the puppy does not have to worry about being corrected for playing chase. To the puppy, it is just a game. They played the same game when they were with their littermates. Chase, as has been stated before, is a dog's favorite game. Whether chasing cars, people, or other animals, it is still a game to the dog. There is something moving, and it must be caught. Use this chase drive to your advantage when teaching the "come" command.

Your dog should have a confined area where it can exercise and release some of the day's frustrations. It should not be allowed to roam about the streets freely. Freedom of movement to roam the streets is the biggest cause of a dog's chasing problem. If the dog is allowed to roam about, there is no one to correct its bad actions. The dog assumes that since no one stopped him, it is okay to do it. The major problem with this is either your dog will end up dead under the tires of an unsuspecting motorist or it will end up biting someone. Neither of these scenarios is going to be good for the dog, your neighbors, or you.

Chasers learn this game at an early age. As with most problems, it is harder to correct the problem after the dog has become accustomed to getting away with it; therefore, it is better to correct it early in the dog's life than to wait.

To stop this situation, place your dog on a six-foot lead. Have a friend drive by you in a car while you are walking your dog. As your dog starts to go for the car, have your friend throw a shake can from the car. (A shake can is a soft-drink can with ten pennies inside, sealed with tape.) As the can hits the ground, change your direction of travel away from the car rapidly, and say nothing to the dog. As the noise is made by the can, you are going in the opposite direction, and the dog does not have time to figure out what just happened. Perform the scenario two or three more times, in different locations. Continue this for about a week or two. Sometimes this takes a little longer, depending on how long your dog has been chasing objects. Do not test the dog off lead, and do not allow him out to chase anything while you are not there to correct the action.

When you see the dog begin to make the adjustment to leave the car alone and change direction on his own while on lead, you may then set him up for an off-lead trial. Do not make this trial until the dog is attempting to make the change while on lead.

There are some other methods used, which include throwing choke chains and/or water-filled balloons from a moving car and banging the side of the car as it goes by. With any of these methods, you should have your dog on his lead so that you may make the correction of changing direction at the same time as the distraction.

Jumping

Puppy

This is one of those things that is found to be really cute as a puppy and totally undesirable as an adult dog. Why wait to train your dog not to jump on you? Start now! When your puppy attempts to jump on you, step directly into him and say nothing to him. This may topple him over, but he will think he misjudged his jump. When he tries again, do the same thing. Continue until he stops jumping, and then have him sit whenever he comes to you. When he sits, give him the attention he wants. In other words, make him work for the attention. By jumping on you, he is demanding attention. Teach him that he will get attention if he sits in front of you. If you discourage the jumping as a puppy, you will not have to worry about his jumping on you as an adult. He will understand the rule and follow the procedure.

I have had people tell me that they have tried this and it does not work. Yes it does. You have to be more persistent than the puppy. He will tire much faster than you will. Stay with it, and you will be rewarded with a dog that does not jump on you. You must be consistent and persistent if you are to succeed.

Another method of stopping this action is to step on his rear toes. Do not step so hard that you hurt him, but use just enough pressure to make it uncomfortable. When he gets off, command him to sit. Then praise him for sitting.

Do not talk to the dog while he is jumping on you, or when you are making the correction. You want the dog to think that whatever is happening to him is his fault. He is the cause of his falling over or his feet being stepped on. When he perceives the problem to be one he has caused, he will stop jumping. If you allow the dog to see a correction coming from you, he will avoid the correction by jumping on your side or back. Never let him see the correction coming. Make him believe he caused the problem. Proof of this can be seen when looking back on what the puppy has gone through. Remember that puppy walk? It is the walk you performed when you first got your puppy. You would step totally out of your way to prevent stepping on him because he was always underfoot. Then the day came that you did not see him, and you stepped on his foot. From that day forward, he never got underfoot again. It is the same principle, without all the pain.

Do not put your hands on the dog to push him away. Placing your hands on your dog is, to him, a sign of approval, and the action will continue. Using your hands to push him away will only have him think that you approve of his actions or that you want to play. Placing your hands on your dog, even when correcting him, is a sign of approval from you.

Adult

The dog that jumps on people is one of the most common complaints. It all begins with the puppy. We allow the puppy to jump on us, and we lie on the floor and let him crawl over us. Then, when we are tired of it, we want him to understand that it's not fun anymore. At least it is not fun for us. When a dog jumps up, most people will put their hands on the dog and push him away. What they have just done is praise him for jumping, because they have placed their hands on him. Keep in mind that this is what is done to praise the dog. He accepts your placing your hands on him as a sign that it is acceptable behavior and that you approve of the action, even though you are trying to prevent his jumping on you.

To correct this problem, begin by allowing the dog jump up. When his head is above your knee, place your knee into his chest firmly. Do not try to knock him out, just cause some discomfort. The key to making this method work is for the dog not to see the correction. If you allow his head to rise above your knee prior to making the correction, he thinks that he has caused the discomfort. If he sees you trying to knee him, he will know that you are the force behind the discomfort, and he will change his strategy. He will begin jumping from the side, from behind, or both. Let the correction be a surprise to him, and do not let him see it coming.

Correcting in this manner will take only two or three times to make him think before jumping on you. If you want to use a command in conjunction with the action, say "Off." Once he is off, do not touch him. You may talk to him and ask him what happened, but do not touch him or repeat the command. When he is giving the indication that he wants to jump but does not, give him the command to sit. When he sits, then you may touch and praise him, but do not allow him to jump up from that position.

If your dog is too small for you to use your knee, try stepping on his rear toes when he jumps on you. Do not crush the toes; simply step on them enough to have him move off of you. He will realize that every time he gets on you, it is uncomfortable, and he will stop jumping up.

No matter who the dog jumps on, the correction must be applied by the individual. This technique usually takes two to three instances for the dog to begin to understand that jumping on people is uncomfortable. One week of training is the longest I have ever seen a dog continue jumping before ending the action. I believe the reason to be that the family was not enforcing the correction as a unit, and the dog was confused.

Getting on Furniture

Another complaint is that the dog will not stay off the sofa or bed. Well, if the floor were so comfortable, we would be sleeping on it. Of course the dog wants to get up there! It is where most of your scent is located, and he wants to be there also. Besides, it is nice and soft.

This rule is the same as for jumping. You must be persistent and not let him on these items at any time. This includes that cute, cuddly, little puppy. If you are holding him while you are on the bed, sofa, or that favorite chair, you are teaching him that it is okay to be there. Then, when you decide that you want your chair, he tells you with a grunt or growl that you are disturbing his rest. After all, you told him when he was younger that it was okay to be there. If you do not want a dog on your furniture, start by forbidding the puppy.

Okay, so you did not tell him it was okay, and you did not give those underlying signals. The approach you take here is to pull him off the furniture by his collar and command "Off." This action must be performed swiftly. Do not start commanding from one side of the room and approach the dog. This would only give him a warning that you are coming to make a correction, and put him on guard for your action. The action must be performed swiftly and without warning. Simply walk to the dog, grab the collar, command "Off," and pull him off the furniture. Do not give the command and wait to see if the dog will comply, and do not linger when the command is given. It must be done swiftly to be effective. When he is off the item, do not praise him for getting off, but make him sit in front of you. Praise him, both verbally and physically, for sitting, not for getting off the furniture.

If he is the type that will get on the furniture while you are in another room and jump off when you enter his area, you need another approach. Try taping balloons on the furniture. It will serve to confuse him, and if he does jump on them, they will pop. The sound will frighten him, he will have made his own correction, and he will stay away from the furniture.

Another method is the shake can. Use an aluminum soft-drink can and place ten to fifteen pennies inside. Use just enough to give the can enough weight so it can be thrown. Once the stones or pennies are inside, tape the opening with duct tape. When you catch him in the act, throw the can. It will make enough noise to scare him, and, if he is hit with the can, he will not be hurt. Keep in mind that you are training your dog. Do not allow your frustration to reach a point where you are trying to "knock the dog out of him." After a few of these throws, he will recognize the sound, and you will only have to shake the can for him to understand that he must stop his action.

Barking

Barking is not a problem. It is a means of voicing excitement, joy, and/or a warning. Dogs cannot speak our language, so they try to communicate using their language. In fact, barking can be used to aid you if you want a dog that will let you know when there is danger or some disturbance about the house.

Incessant barking is a problem. Generally, this type of barking is caused by boredom or insufficient exercise. Dogs that are not socialized with people or other animals will also acquire this trait.

If you have not socialized your dog with others outside of the home, then begin taking him for walks around the neighborhood or in the shopping center parking lot, where he is not on his territory. This action has calmed many dogs. Being away from their territory, they are not sure of what to expect, and are more dependent on your actions. Have strangers come up to him and pet him. If he is still out of control in these areas, then place him in an obedience class where he will learn various commands. These commands will help to give you the appearance of being the alpha authority, and your dog will calm down.

Obedience training is not just for the show dog. Its aim is to teach him some manners. That is what obedience classes teach. Your dog learns manners and understands that you are the authority, not him.

A barking dog cannot hear your voice, because there is a flap on the inside of the ear that closes up when it is barking. This is similar to your putting your fingers in your ears. You can hear the sound, but it is muffled. You have to break through the barking level and reach the inner ear with a noise that will penetrate the closed flap.

I have found water to be one of the easiest ways to get a grip on this problem. If your dog lives outdoors and has a confined area, you may use a hose. When the barking starts, give the command "Quiet" and spray him directly in the face with the water. I know there are dogs that love the water, but I have not found one yet that likes a full stream of water hitting him in the face. You may have to do this a number of times, but if you are persistent, you will have a dog that understands what "quiet" means. After a time, the shake can will be enough to get their attention.

If your dog is a house dog, you do not want to use a water hose, but use a water gun or spray bottle. Use the same procedure, only substitute the water gun or spray bottle for the hose. Give the command, make a noise, and squirt the water in his face. You may try adding a teaspoonful of vinegar to the water. This sometimes helps discourage barking.

Distraction from what he is doing is the only way you are going to achieve results. If you are frustrated and do not distract him first, you are wasting your time. He must be distracted from what is causing the barking before you can make any corrections. In the home, you do not want to run around the house with a water gun all day, so use the shake can. You can throw the can to distract him from the barking or any offensive action. Being made of soft aluminum, if the can hits him, it will not hurt him, but the noise will definitely get his attention. Then give him the command to "Quiet" or whatever command you prefer.

Coprophagia

This is the scientific name for "stool eating." As disgusting as it appears, the dog does not seem to mind the taste, and it will not do him any harm. It is not the greatest form of protein, but it does contain a certain amount of protein. Indirectly, it could be stool from a dog that is infected with a disease or internal parasite, and that could cause future problems.

Spraying stool with "no-chew" products or covering it with pepper or hot sauce to stop the dog from eating it is futile. If you have the time to spray, you have the time to pick it up. Removal of the stool and keeping his area in a sanitary condition are the major elements in correcting this problem.

There are various opinions as to why this habit develops. Some schools of thought are that whelping females through weeks of cleaning up after their puppies will develop this as a habit. Some dietary studies indicate dogs suffering a deficiency in their diet will begin this habit. Before you make any changes in their diet or attempt to correct the problem, have your dog checked by a veterinarian to be certain that there are not any hidden physical problems. If the dog checks out okay, try feeding him twice a day instead of once. Give him just enough food in the two feedings that will equal the amount of food had he been fed once. Often, the two feedings will give the dog a full feeling and deter this habit. Be careful not to overfeed your dog, or he will have a problem with diarrhea.

The quality of the food you are feeding could be the cause also. If the food you are feeding does not have the proper nutrients in it, the dog will eat its stool, trying to regain the nutrients it is missing. It could also be that the food is not satisfying the dog's hunger. This can be avoided by feeding a good-quality dry dog food containing enough protein and fat to satisfy the dog and maintain his optimal weight.

Boredom is another reason for this habit. Be sure that your dog receives enough exercise and socialization. Take him for a walk or spend some time playing with him in the yard. There is no sure way of ending this habit other than to make it unavailable to him. Cleaning any stool from the yard daily is a must. Do not leave stool lying around the yard. If it isn't there, he can't eat it.

If all of the above precautions have been taken and your dog has reached the habitual stage, you may try: 1) sprinkling about one teaspoonful of Adolph's meat tenderizer on his food each day for approximately five days, or 2) add a heaping tablespoonful of canned pumpkin to his food. Pumpkin will add fiber to his diet, and the transition from intake to output seems to cause a protein change, and the dog may be discouraged by the bitter taste of the waste. If you have more than one dog, you will have to treat all of their food at the same time.

Above all, no matter which method you choose, you should clean your yard and pens daily. Never leave stool lying around. It can lead to other problems within your dog, and it could be transferred to your family.

Fighting

Before explaining how to separate dogs that are fighting, it should be noted that this should never be attempted by the novice handler. It takes practice and timing, and if it is done incorrectly, the handlers will be bitten. You should never attempt to break up a fight alone. Doing so will only bring you serious injury.

It also bears mentioning that most states have a leash law, which states that all dogs should be on a leash anytime they are off of their property or outside of their enclosure.

Most fighting problems can be resolved by socialization. Keeping a dog locked away from outside activities and from mingling with other dogs is a major cause of dogfights.

When two dogs meet, one is going to be the more dominant dog. If the other does not submit or show signs of submission, or accept the other as the alpha figure, the fight will begin. Long before there were any teeth shown, the fight began, and you probably did not notice it.

First, the dog will assume a stiff, proud-looking posture. This is a sign of dominance. Next, he will stretch himself up on his toes. This is to make him appear taller than he actually is. If there is no submissive sign, he will raise his hackles. Hackles are the hairs you see standing up on the back of his neck. Some dogs will raise the hair along the length of their backs. At this point, the fight is about to begin. The fight will not begin at ground level, but in the air. One or both will leap into the air, and toward the other dog in order to be on top of the attack. The reason for leaping into the air is to make them appear even taller, and to have the advantage of being on top.

The problematic solution most people use in separating two fighting dogs is to pull backward on the lead. Pulling backwards raises the dog even higher and escalates the fight. To break up a fight, slide your hand halfway down the lead, forcing your dog into a submissive posture, and pull him out of the fight. When he goes down and out, the other dog will back off, thinking he has won. If both handlers respond in like manner, the fight is over, no one is hurt, and who cares what the other dog thinks?

With dogs fighting that are not on lead, you have to intervene as the alpha figure. The following technique must be performed rapidly and without any hesitation, or you will be bitten. Never attempt to grab the collar of a fighting dog. First, the dog will feel that you are attempting to get into the fight, and you could be bitten. Secondly, the dog is in such a heightened state of defense, it will not recognize that you are attempting to assist. Placing your hand close to the working end of a fighting dog is an invitation for the dog to bite.

Once again, I caution you with using this procedure. It requires two people, so do not attempt this on your own. Grab the dog by his rear legs, and raise him up so that he is standing on his front legs only. As you do this, begin making circles with the dog. Continue circling until you reach an area where you can get control of your dog. Do not stop circling or let go of the dog. If you stop circling, he will reach back and bite you. If you release him, he will re-engage in the fight.

Once he has been removed from the fight, attach his lead to his collar, or loop it around his neck so that you will have control and prevent him from re-engaging. It is best to turn the dogs away from each other so there is no eye contact. When you have him turned and settled, give the down command. The more submissive dog will then have the opportunity to run or walk away from the fight. There may be some growling and grumbling, but ignore it as long as you have control of the dog.

Dogs, like their wolf cousins, do not end a fight in this manner. The victor of any fight is the first to leave the scene. If the loser were to attempt to leave, the fight would continue until the loser was in a submissive posture, lying on the ground. Then the victor would leave the scene, watching that the opponent did not get up until a proper distance had been acquired. This is the most important reason for holding on to your dog. You are allowing the loser to flee the fight, and the aggressor knows instinctively that he has proven his authority.

Correcting this problem takes time, and a variety of methods must be used. After the dog has been trained and the fighting curtailed, that dog should not be trusted to be alone in any situation that would provoke a fight, because he will answer the call.

Escaping

The digger or tunnel expert that makes his escape by digging a hole under the fence must be discouraged from digging. This may be done by attaching chicken wire to the fence and burying it. You will need to purchase enough chicken wire (twenty-four inches wide) to completely encompass the inside perimeter of your fence. Dig a trench around the inside of the fence approximately six to eight inches deep. Attach the wire to the bottom of your fence, bend it, and allow the rest to lay flat in the trench. Cover the wire by refilling the trench. Pack the dirt down as much as possible.

Chicken wire is inexpensive and causes great discomfort to diggers as it gets between their toes while they are digging. This discomfort will generally stop the digging to escape.

If he digs up a portion of the fence, re-bury it as soon as possible. It may take a week or two, but your dog will stop digging under the fence. If the fence is low enough, he may begin jumping against the fence to test its height, to estimate his success in going over it.

The jumper is not as difficult to stop as most would believe. If your dog has a habit of jumping the gate, you may try attaching two rods, approximately ten inches in length, on either side of your gate. Between the two rods, stretch some rubber bands about three to four inches apart. Now when the dog jumps, he will hit the rubber bands, which are not readily visible to him. After a few jumps at the gate, the rubber bands will make enough noise and cause discomfort, that he will stop jumping.

The dog cannot see the rubber bands, and when he attempts to jump the gate, the rubber bands distract him. The rubber bands will not hurt him, but the sudden surprise of being grabbed by an unseen object will make him back off. If he has a favorite spot along the fence that he likes jumping over, this method can be used there also.

If he has a favorite place to go over, try placing a shrub or an object that he cannot use as an aid in the same area. Place it approximately two feet away from the fence. This will make his jump start farther back than he would like, and he will stop going over.

Fence-climbers are another problem. You can place plants around the inside of the fence, which makes it harder for him to get to the fence. This may cost you a few plants at first, but eventually, he will stop climbing. Place the plants about a foot inside the fence.

There are electrical devices on the market that do work and will stop the action. The drawback is that you may spend a few hundred dollars, and the system may deter him from climbing, but now he is jumping over the fence. You may run that same wire at ground level and at fence level. This will stop the climbing and jumping, but now you will be susceptible to the same shock as the dog. I have physically tested some of these devices on myself. It was not a pleasant feeling.

If you choose to use one of these devices, use the type that subjects the dog to a direct shock, not the type that is buried underground. For the digger, run the wire approximately six inches off the ground and around the inside of the fence. For the climber or jumper, run the wire approximately four inches above the fence. You will need to purchase the plastic stand-offs that prevent the fence from grounding against the metal.

Once the dog discovers the unpleasant feeling of the wire, he will stay away from the fence. He may run a path about fourteen inches away from the wire, but he will avoid the wire, and the digging, jumping, and/or climbing will end.

One of the common causes of climbing or digging is a lack of exercise. Most owners believe that the dog will get enough exercise by himself and do not take the dog for a walk around the neighborhood. The dog wants to get out, release some energy, and mark the area to claim it as his territory. Exercise will help to keep him in his yard. Another problem is dogs next door or a dog that is in heat. Talk with your neighbors. Find out what dogs are in the neighborhood, and ask those with dogs in heat to lock them up during that time. This will help keep your dog from trying to leave his property to investigate.

Another thing that will cause this action is dogs that are allowed to roam the neighborhood unattended. The temptation of being out with another dog that is not under human control is so great that your dog will do whatever it takes to be with him. Leash laws are very effective in this regard. Keep strays and free-roaming dogs out of your area, and this will help to reduce your problems.

Door Guards

A dog that guards the door by barking the arrival of guests, then growls when they enter the home is attempting to be a leader. He may also display the act of mounting someone's leg. Eventually, he will bite if he is not corrected. This is a territorial problem, and he feels that he is guarding his territory. He does not want this person invading his den.

Start by placing your dog on a lead before you go to the door. If he barks, correct him and place him in a sit. All is well if he quiets down. If he does not, take him away from the door. Place him in his crate or room and lock him up. He must understand that he is not to make threats at the door. Use a command for this action also.

Crate, house, room, bed, and *place* are all good commands. "Go lay down" is not a good command. I like to train the dog to go to a special place in the room. Start by placing a mat or rug in one corner and teach your dog "Place." Take him to the rug, command "place, down, stay." This one command must be broken down into stages. 1) Place—Take him to the rug, so that he understands that you want him to go to this spot when he hears the command "Place." 2) Down— When you arrive at the rug, have him assume a down position. 3) Stay—Once in the down position, command him to stay. This exercise may be learned in as little as five days. You will determine the amount of time the dog stays in his place. The longer you make him stay, the better he will understand. In fact, he will begin to use this spot to lie down when he is not involved in a family activity. When he wants to rest, he will begin to go to his "place" and lie down.

This dog also needs socialization. I cannot overemphasize the importance of socialization.

Chapter 29
Boarding

Wife: "Did you remember that I'm going to a meeting this weekend?"

Husband: "Oh, I forgot about that. I'm taking the boys to the scout camp this weekend."

Wife: "Well, what about the dog?"

Husband: "Gee, see if you can find someone to care for him, or call Bob and ask him what he does with his dog, or check the phone book for boarding kennels. I guess we'll have to board him if we can't find anyone to care for him."

This is just one of the ways dogs and people are introduced to boarding kennels. Something happens at the spur of the moment, the dog does not fit into the plans, and off he goes.

This is not the way to find a boarding kennel. You should take the time to inquire about boarding kennels and interview the owners before you ever need to use them. There are some things that you need to know before you board your dog, and there are some things about your dog that need to be known by the kennel. There are questions that need to be answered before you place your dog somewhere he has never been. I have spent some time interviewing various boarding kennel owners, gathering information on what they felt was important to them and the dog owner. I have assembled a list of things that you should investigate and be aware of prior to going to a boarding kennel.

Shots

Unless you are boarding your dog at your veterinarian's office, you will need your dog's shot record and the telephone number of your veterinarian. The kennel will want to confirm that your dog is up to date on all of his shots and that they were received at least ten days prior to his boarding. All of the kennels that I have interviewed require the dog to have a Bordetella (kennel cough) vaccination. Most will accept the dog on the same day of receiving it if the vaccine was one that was administered intranasally. This vaccine is used to prevent your dog from becoming infected with kennel cough. Kennel cough is similar to the common cold, causing sneezing, runny nose, and coughing. It is highly contagious and can be a serious problem if it is not controlled. This will help to prevent your dog from becoming ill and/or spreading it to others in the kennel.

Pens, Runs, and Cages

You will want to know the sizes of the pen or run where your dog will stay. A minimum of four by ten feet for a medium-sized dog will provide enough room to pace and move around comfortably. In addition to pen size and area, ask if your dog will be exercised outside of his pen. Request a tour of the facility and the kennel area, to be certain he is able to obtain shelter from within his run. If there should be a problem with another boarder, is the facility capable of moving him to another area or pen? There should be enough room at the facility to afford the dogs to be taken out of their pens for exercise, especially if this is going to be a lengthy stay. Some facilities charge extra to walk the dogs outside of the runs, while others include it in the cost of the stay. You must make the request.

Sanitation

The facility should be clean and odor-free. The presence of flies is a good indication that the facility is not being kept to standard. A few flies are going to be present in any facility, but if there is an abundance of them, this is an indicator as to the type of care your dog will be receiving. If there are flies all around as you are touring, I suggest that you find another facility. The pen areas should be cleaned at least twice each day. Ask if the pens are sanitized when a dog is removed. Most will scrub the pen/holding areas with bleach and soap solution. Bleach is excellent for killing germs, but if it is not thoroughly rinsed, it can cause burns on the pads of the feet and the genitals. Do not be afraid to ask. Most of the operators are aware of this problem and take the precautions to rinse thoroughly after a bleach application.

Climate Control

The great majority of the facilities I viewed are designed so the dog has an exercise area that is exposed and an enclosed area that is cooled and/or heated. This affords the dog the option of staying in an outside environment or entering into an enclosed one. Some facilities were outdoor runs where the runs were covered and the dog had access to a house within the run.

Escapes

Ask if there have ever been any escapes. Almost every kennel I have talked with had experienced an escape artist, and accidents do happen. There should be a fenced area to protect the dog from leaving the facility if he should escape the hands of one of the personnel or finds a way out of his pen. These areas are used for exercising your dog and keeping him within the confines of the facility. Inquire as to whether they have ever lost a dog that was being boarded. You want to be sure that the security afforded by the kennel will protect your dog, so that he will be waiting for you when you return.

Personnel

Do not assume that the personnel you see have been trained. Ask what type of training has been provided to the personnel who will be handling your dog, and who trains them. You want to know how many personnel are being utilized to maintain the facility and who will be there after closing. The number of personnel will indicate the capability of the operator to fulfill his promise of keeping your dog and ensuring his safety. The qualifications of those personnel will give you the assurance that they will know what to look for when tending to the animals. That training will enable them to identify an injury, health problem, or any changes in the dog's demeanor. Early notice helps to prevent minor problems from becoming more serious ones.

Veterinarians

Is there a veterinarian on call to this facility? I found that most of the facilities try to accommodate their clients by using the same veterinarian as the dog's owner. They would rather use a veterinarian who is familiar with the dog than utilize another. There are circumstances where your veterinarian may be too far away for them to transport your dog, and in those instances, they will utilize a standby veterinarian available to them. Inquire as to which veterinarians are used and if there is an emergency clinic in the area. There are after-hours clinics, and some veterinarians will take after-hours calls. You will want the comfort of knowing that your dog will be cared for in the same manner that you would care for him. If you want to be notified of care before it is given, you will have to give a location where you may be contacted. I have found it best to let the kennel operator make the decision. In an emergency, time is the most important factor, and when searching for an owner who is out of town can waste a lot of valuable time.

Food

Your dog will be placed on the feeding schedule of the kennel. If this is a problem, it should be addressed when you sign in. If your dog requires a different schedule than the one they are using, you should notify them. This may cost a little extra, but your dog will be maintained in the manner to which he is accustomed. After all, if everybody had a special request, it would take more personnel to run the establishment and cost more to board your dog.

Ask what kinds of foods are available. Most keep a variety of foods, but it may not be what you want. If your dog requires a special food, or, if you do not want to switch to the food they are using, you will have to provide them with food. There may be an extra charge for this. Look at it from their standpoint. A program of feeding has been established, and the introduction of a different food interrupts the flow of that program.

A change in foods will sometime cause gastric distress that will last for a few days. When your dog returns home, he may undergo that same distress when he is placed back on the food he had prior to boarding. Do not be alarmed that something has happened to your dog while you were away. It is the sudden changes in diet that cause this problem, and it will resolve itself in a few days. You may want to ask the kennel operator for some of the food they are using so the change may be made slowly and avoid any gastric problems.

Special Requests

If your dog is taking medication or needs something administered in your absence, you must make it known prior to leaving. Some operators charge extra to administer medication and some do not.

If you want your dog cleaned or groomed prior to picking him up, you will have to make those arrangements also. There will be a charge for washing and/or grooming.

Some establishments employ trainers to exercise the dogs and instruct basic obedience. If this is something that you would like, you must inquire about it. This is another charge.

Hours

Ask about the normal operating hours. When will you be able to drop off and pick up your dog? Ask if anyone is available for pick-up or drop-off after hours or on Sundays and holidays. Some establishments will not open for regular business on a Sunday or a holiday. Some charge extra for after-hours, Sunday, and holiday business.

Cost

Know the cost of leaving your dog. The fees are generally established by weight and/or size. The larger your dog, the higher the daily cost. Will you need to leave a deposit? Most operators ask for a deposit, because there have been occasions where a stray dog has been dropped off under the pretense of being boarded and then left there. Now the operator is left with the responsibility of taking care of this situation.

If you plan on a lengthy stay, ask if there are special rates for those stays. Usually there is some break in the scheduled fees when the dog will stay for extended periods; however, most operators will want the first two weeks paid in advance. Be prepared for this.

Ask if they accept credit cards, and if they do, which ones. Some do not accept any type of credit cards.

Security

Inquire about security personnel. Are there any cameras in use? Is each pen/run locked or fashioned so that the dog cannot open the gate? Is the facility locked so there cannot be any access while they are away? These will add the peace of mind that your dog is being protected.

Insurance

Inquire about liability insurance. You will want to know if the facility is carrying insurance to protect your dog. There may be insurance covering the loss of the buildings and their contents. Do they carry insurance to protect your dog while he is being boarded? The insurance policy should include your dog. They may never have had a problem, but if one develops, you want to know that your dog is protected and the situation can be handled without distress or recourse.

This should help you on your way to finding a good boarding kennel, and make your pet's stay there a pleasant one. Knowing these things in advance will help give you the peace of mind that your pet is being cared for properly while you are away. In addition, you will know what to expect upon your return.

Your Dog

You will want to know if there is any interaction between the personnel and your dog throughout the day. Remember, your dog is going to be in a strange place, and this could be stressful to him. Interaction with him will help to calm and assure him that he is safe. Interaction with each dog takes time, and you will want to know what amount of time is being spent with him, and what type of interaction is being performed. When there is interaction with the dogs in a facility, the operator is given a better opportunity to catch any problems far in advance of their becoming serious ones.

Chapter 30
Traveling

Boarding your dog while you are on vacation may not be appealing to you. You may want to have your dog accompany you. There are many people who take their dogs with them when camping, hiking, and vacationing. Before you decide that your dog should be with you, you should consider a few things.

Does your dog travel without getting carsick? Carsickness is simply motion sickness and is not a pleasant thing to have to contend with while you are traveling. There are medications to aid your dog in controlling carsickness. Most medications will make the dog drowsy and somewhat lethargic, and the effects of the medication could last longer than you would desire. Before giving your dog any over-the-counter medications, check with your veterinarian to ensure the dog's safety and be aware of any side effects of the medication.

If carsickness is not a problem for your dog, will you be able to tolerate the barking and moving about inside the car when he sees something of interest to him? You know, like when he sees the neighborhood cat and wants to get at it. While on vacation, he is going to encounter many varying situations, as well as other people and animals. A dog barking inside a closed vehicle can be an ear-piercing sound, which could distract you from your driving.

If your dog is one that travels well, you are only halfway there. You should ensure that the motels accept dogs. Most motels will not allow a dog to remain unrestrained or unattended inside the room, but many will allow them to stay if they are kept inside a crate. This means you will have to pack your dog's crate and take it along with your baggage. Those motels that allow dogs to remain in the room have a policy about keeping the dog quiet. If he is a barker, he will have to go.

Some motels provide kennels where you may keep your dog. This is very convenient, but with this setup, there are many unknowns. You do not know the dogs that may have been in there before your dog. Were their vaccinations current? Could they have been in with a contagious disease? Who maintains the kennels? Were they sanitized after each use? Do you want to take that chance?

It is best to inquire in advance when taking your dog with you on vacation. You may have to plan your route around the motels that will accept dogs. Ask if there is a deposit required for the dog to stay. Some motels require a deposit from $5 to $50 per dog for dogs staying in the room, crated or not.

You will need to take food and water along for your dog. You may not always find the type of food you are feeding your dog in other areas. Changing his food at this time would not be a good idea. Rapid food changes can cause your dog to develop diarrhea, and this is not very pleasant for you or the dog. The water your dog has become accustomed to is also important. You do not know what chemicals are in the drinking water in other areas, and they could have an adverse effect on your dog's system. Bottled water is often a good choice, since it is supposed to be bottled without additives.

Traveling by car is the way most people get around these days. When traveling interstate, you must have a health certificate dated less than ten days prior, signed by a veterinarian, stating that your dog is up to date on all of his shots. Some states require you to stop at checkpoints along the highways and let them inspect your pet and your paperwork.

The agricultural departments of some states are set up to monitor such things as dogs, horses, and plants brought into their area. They have vehicles to patrol the highways and have the authority to stop you for an inspection of your paperwork. If everything is not in order, they have the authority to impound your dog.

Traveling with your dog also means that you must monitor him closely. You may have to make unscheduled stops because your dog is ready to relieve himself. Some dogs will wait, while others will not. You must be patient and not try to rush him. There are all kinds of foreign odors around him that need investigating, and he has to choose just the right spot.

A health and safety precaution that you may want to use is to carry a spray bottle containing a bleach solution of one tablespoon of bleach to eight ounces of water. Before getting back into the car, spray the dog's feet and wipe his nose with a cloth sprayed with the solution. This is mild enough not to cause any burns, but strong enough to kill the bacteria he may have contacted while out of the car.

If you are planning to travel by plane, your dog will need a health certificate dated not more than ten days prior to your departure. You must have an airline-approved crate for your dog's travel. The crate must be large enough for him to stand and turn around without hitting his head. There must be food and water containers attached to the crate. Your dog will travel in the baggage compartment of the plane, so it is best to inquire about the baggage compartment's environmental controls. Most airlines have pressurized baggage compartments, but not all are climate controlled. Do not make any assumptions. Ask the questions!

If you want to keep your dog in the passenger compartment with you, he must be in a crate that will fit under your seat. If the crate will not fit under the seat, you will have to buy a seat for the dog. It will cost the same price as your ticket, but your dog will have its own seat.

The only exceptions to this rule are search-and-rescue and guide dogs. These dogs are allowed to travel on the plane next to their handler.

Ask your veterinarian if he is familiar with the areas in which you will be traveling. Does he know of any facilities or other veterinarians in those areas? There may not be any problems with your dog, but if one occurs, it is nice to know that you will have someone who was referred to you by your own veterinarian.

Many people take their dogs along on vacation and enjoy themselves. I do not want to discourage you from taking your dog with you. I just want you to know some of the things you need to consider before taking your dog. I hope this has been helpful.

Chapter 31
Breeding

More times than not, owners contemplate breeding their dogs for reasons that can be proven false. I have heard many reasons for breeding, one of which is, "I just want to breed him/her one time so that they will mature." I do not know where this idea came from, but I disagree with it completely. What happens to the dogs that are born sterile? Do they ever mature? Of course they do. Breeding your dog is not going to make your dog mature. Time and experience will make him mature.

There are more risks with breeding a dog than not, such as the stress of carrying, delivering, and nursing the puppies. Infections such as mastitis can cause serious complications when nursing the pups, and even more trouble for the female because she will require treatment with antibiotics to clear up the infection. The complications of delivering puppies could endanger the dog's life. Health problems may develop and remain after the puppies are gone. There are complications that no one can predict. On top of that, there probably have not been any plans to place the puppies when they arrive. Now the owner realizes that he has these little bundles of fluff that must go to new homes, because he cannot afford to keep all those puppies. The search begins, and usually a puppy will end up in another home because someone wanted to help a friend. Then, about a year later, they no longer want the puppy, and it will end up in a shelter.

Some owners acquire dogs with good pedigrees, with the thought that they can breed this dog to make money. If you think you are going to make a lot of money doing this, let me put you on the right path. By the time you are finished with examinations and shots for your dog, veterinarian visits to check the puppies, worming, shots for the puppies, food, the time that goes into caring for and socializing the puppies, you will be lucky if you have enough money left to pay the food bill. If you want to take a chance on making some money, buy a lottery ticket. Your chances of becoming rich are much better, and you will not be adding to the overcrowding in the shelters.

It makes much more sense to spay or neuter your pet. They do not have to produce or sire a litter to mature. Allowing your dog to breed does not solve or expedite anything. In fact, in some cases it can cause more problems. If you intend to spay/neuter after the litter, what makes you think the dog will not remember the experience it encountered? What makes you believe that it will not try to breed again? If spay/neuter is what you intend to do, then do it when the dog reaches six months of age. Spaying your female will help prevent pyometria, or cancer of the mammary glands, and neutering your male will prevent testicular cancer, thus extending the life of your pet.

Okay, so you think you have the best of the best. Well, you had better sit down and do some homework. Just because you have a dog that has a champion bloodline going back to his ancestors' arrival on the *Mayflower* does not mean that he will produce champion dogs. It does not take champions to produce champions. It takes the right combination of genes to align themselves to produce that special dog. If you intend to breed, first study canine genetics. You must know what you may be producing. Will you know all the answers? No, but you will have a better idea of what is about to take place and what you can expect from breeding your dog, in order to avoid some of the pitfalls. In addition, you must know the bloodlines of the mate you intend to use. You must know what kind of puppies have developed from this line of dogs. What were their temperaments? What is the temperament of the breeding pair? How sound is their skeletal structure? What diseases may be developed? What genetic deficiencies may be produced? The list of possible problems goes on.

Although the dogs that are seen on major televised dog shows influence many people in their decisions to purchase a particular breed, more information is needed. Oh yes, those are some handsome dogs, but how many dogs have they competed against that did not make the final show? No one considers that there is competition all along the way before a dog reaches this level. What do you ever hear about those other dogs?

I am not trying to discourage you from breeding if you have done all of your homework on the subject, but I am trying to make you aware that it takes a great deal of time and work to produce a dog that will reach this level. One must also consider that this is only one dog. What happened to his littermates?

I do not know the percentages of dogs that reach the higher levels, but I can assure you that they are in the lower range. I am not just talking about "show" dogs. I am speaking of field-trial champions and working dogs as well. Some dogs are utilized to hunt, work, and protect livestock, and guard businesses, and some are used by law-enforcement agencies. If you were to take all of these dogs together, you would only have a small portion of the entire dog world. There are more dogs kept as pets than are used for any other purpose. With this being the case, you should realize that there are enough dogs out there without you adding to them for the sheer pleasure of seeing puppies being born.

If breeding is what you want, please put the time and energy into establishing a list of people interested in a puppy before you ever decide to breed. Have a home for these puppies to go to, and be certain that those taking a puppy understand what will be required to maintain it. Puppies grow up, and oftentimes once the fun is gone, so is the dog. Try to get to know the person who is getting one of your puppies. If you feel that a person is not suited to have one of your puppies, do not place it with them. Believe me, they will find another dog somewhere. You want people who care about your puppies and the life of the dog.

I am a breeder of Louisiana Catahoula Leopard Dogs, and have denied ownership of my puppies to people I felt did not fit the criteria for owning one. I will not breed any of my females unless there are a minimum of six deposits for puppies to ensure the placement of those puppies being born. If there are not enough people waiting for a puppy, then the female will not breed.

Prior to breeding, you must investigate the background of the pair. You must check the litters that they came from, and the litters before that, to ensure that there are no genetic anomalies or problems that could be reproduced. All of this takes time and study.

As a breeder, you must be prepared for anything. Do you know what to do when the pups start to arrive? Are you prepared for an emergency? Do you know who to call and where to go if your dog should have problems delivering? There are any number of problems that could occur during delivery, or the inability to deliver normally. When this occurs, you had better know what to do, or you will not only lose your puppies, you could lose your dog.

There are times when a puppy will not be wanted by anyone. What will you do with it? Where will it stay? You have to be prepared to keep that puppy until someone decides that they would like to have it. You also have to be able to accept that there are going to be some defective puppies that should be destroyed. Are you prepared to take that pup to your veterinarian and pay the cost of destroying the pup? Can you accept it?

In addition to those possibilities above, what will you do if one or more of the persons who took a puppy from you decides that they no longer want or can care for it? Are you willing to take it back? Will you have the space and finances to care for those that are returned, or will you be adding to the bulging sides of animal shelters around the country, and complaining that your tax dollars are being spent frivolously?

I just want you to think about what you are undertaking, should you decide that you want to breed your dog. There is more work involved in breeding *good* dogs than just putting a pair of dogs together and waiting for Mother Nature to take her course.

If you have decided that you are willing and able to undergo the breeding of your dog, then you should study the process and know it inside and out. Even if you own the stud, there are things you need to know before you allow him to breed. Tests need to be performed on both male and female prior to breeding, to ensure that there are no diseases that could render both of them useless for breeding in the future. Think before you breed!

Chapter 32
First Aid for Dogs

Prior to the occurrence of any emergency, you should know your veterinarian's telephone number and office location, as well as the location of the after-hours emergency facility. Most veterinarians have a referral office that they recommend using when the vet is not at his clinic. This information could make a difference in your dog's life. First aid is not a substitute for a visit to your veterinarian. Once the emergency has been tended to, you should definitely visit this office.

As you begin to administer first aid, have someone contact the veterinarian and apprise him of the situation and the procedure you are performing. Time is the most important factor when administering first aid. You must utilize the necessary action in as timely a manner as possible, and then transport the dog to the veterinarian's location.

Providing first aid to an injured animal requires the utmost of caution to prevent further injury to the dog, and to prevent being bitten while attempting to perform the required task. Placing a muzzle on the dog in these situations is always advisable. If a muzzle is not available, one can be fashioned from a dog's lead or a piece of cord. Using a dog lead, hold one end alongside the dog's muzzle, and make two wraps around the nose. This will have each end of the lead on either side of the dog's muzzle and pointed toward the feet. Tie the ends of the lead around the back of the dog's neck securely, and the dog will not be able to bite.

Another method that works well, especially on short-muzzled dogs, is to place a towel or similar material over their head and hold both ends firmly to the ground. This prevents the dog from any visual or physical contact, and will usually calm him.

The following is listed alphabetically, and not the order of importance.

Allergic Reactions

Allergies may occur from certain foods, insect bites, or plants. A redness of the skin or tiny bumps appearing on the skin is an indication of an allergic reaction. Administering Benadryl at ½ mg per pound of body weight will help ease the reaction and any itching that may occur.

Any reaction that includes watery and itchy eyes, sneezing, breathing difficulty, and any swelling or unconsciousness should be considered **severe.** Severe reactions must be handled by a veterinarian.

Bleeding

Minor cuts and scratches may be flushed with betadine or chlorhexidine solutions—or clean, warm water, if these are not available. Flush the area to ensure that all foreign debris has been removed, and apply a triple antibiotic ointment. Bandage if necessary.

Severe or deep lacerations include heavy bleeding and possible injury to ligaments, tendons, and muscles. Using a clean cloth or gauze, apply firm pressure directly to the wound. If possible, bandage the area and transport to the veterinarian.

Internal bleeding requires immediate veterinary care. Symptoms such as rapid breathing, weak pulse, or fainting are indicators of internal bleeding. Blood may be visible in urine or feces, and occasionally around the nose or mouth.

Bloat

Bloat is the second leading cause of death in dogs, after cancer. Bloat may be seen in two forms: *gastric dilatation* and *gastric dilatation-volvulus*. Gastric dilatation is a simple form, referring to a distended stomach filled with air, and requiring decompression with a stomach tube. Gastric dilatation-volvulus is a more severe form in which the stomach swells and rotates between the esophagus and upper intestine, requiring immediate emergency surgery in order to prevent death. Larger breeds are more susceptible to bloat, but the condition has been recorded in other breeds. Common contributors to bloat are: stress; eating habits, such as gulping food; running after a meal; and heredity.

Symptoms include: frequent attempts to vomit, hunching up his back, coughing, heavy salivating, whining, pacing, a drum-tight abdomen, and refusal to lie down, to name a few.

Breathing Problems (CPR)

Cardiopulmonary Resuscitation (CPR) may be administered to a dog that is not breathing. Place the dog on his right side with his head extended in line with his neck. Open the jaws and remove any obstructions. Keeping his mouth closed, cup your hands around his muzzle so that only the nostrils may be seen. Blow three to five quick breaths into the nostrils, and repeat one breath every three seconds. If breathing does not resume, place your hands one on top of the other against the chest and give ten quick compressions, approximately every ten seconds. Continue to switch from nose to chest until breathing resumes. If there are two people present, have one provide the compressions while the other provides the breathing. Once breathing resumes, you should seek immediate veterinary care.

Burns

Burns should be treated with cold or tepid water only. The use of topical solutions or medications without the guidance of a veterinarian could create an infectious wound by locking in germs.

Choking

First, open the jaws to see if there is anything in there that can be removed quickly. If you don't find anything lodged in the mouth, or if you cannot remove the object, you must perform the same maneuver that is used on humans. If your dog is large to medium in size, place him on his back and place the heel of your hand on his stomach, just below the last rib. Place your other hand on top of the hand that is on the dog, and **thrust down and forward** sharply. Continue until the object is expelled.

With smaller breeds, you may place them in your lap with the head pointed toward your knees and apply the same method, using your fingers instead of your whole hand.

Foot Injuries

Most foot injuries are related to the footpad, where suturing is impractical. Ensure that the bleeding has ceased, or apply pressure directly to the wound until it does. Clean the wound, and apply a thin line of super glue, or similar product, to either side of the injury, and hold it together until dried. Bandaging is advisable, but not necessary.

Fractures

Fractures must be stabilized by the use of a rigid splint. Splints can be fashioned from sticks, fishing rods if on a boat, or any rigid item, and must be of a length that extends **above and below** the injury. Wrap the splint with gauze or tape, ensuring that there is blood flow to the lower portion of the injury.

Gunshot Wounds

Immediate veterinary care is required for gunshot wounds, whether a major or minor injury occurs. A minor gunshot wound would be one where the dog is hit by pellets from a shotgun blast from a relatively far distance. The closer he is to the blast, the more serious the wound. The more life-threatening injuries are caused by handguns and rifles, due to the velocity of the missile. Splintered bone and cartilage can cause an internal infection. Control the bleeding and seek immediate veterinary care.

Head Injuries

Any head injury causing unconsciousness requires veterinary care. Place a muzzle on the dog, and keep his head cool with a damp cloth while he is being transported. Disorientation upon waking is common, and owner recognition is not always a probability. The muzzle will avoid your being bitten, should he awaken prior to reaching the veterinarian.

Heatstroke

Rapid panting, red or dry nostrils, increased heartbeat, vomiting, diarrhea, signs of weakness, and disorientation are all signs of heatstroke. The dog must be cooled as quickly as possible. Place him in a tub of water, swimming pool, or pond, and administer electrolytes, such as Pedialyte, until his body temperature is reduced to 103 degrees Fahrenheit. Use a rectal thermometer to obtain the correct body temperature.

Heatstroke may produce serious side effects, including death if left untreated.

Hyperthermia

An overheated dog displaying a widened and lengthened tongue hanging from the mouth, which may have water dripping off of it, is showing signs of hyperthermia. A dripping tongue and wet footprints are indicators of a dog's sweating. Place him in a cool or shaded area, and wipe the areas of the head, neck, and under the legs close to the body with a cool damp cloth. Allow him to drink water, and administer electrolytes.

Hypothermia

A chilled dog curling into a tight ball or seeking shelter is displaying symptoms of hypothermia. He must be warmed slowly by placing him in an area that is shielded from the wind. Place a light blanket over him until he recovers. Rapidly warming him can cause shock. (See **Shock**.)

Hit by Car

Muzzle your dog to prevent being bitten. Attempt to control any profuse bleeding, cover him with a blanket or suitable material, and place him on a rigid board for stability. If there is any dismemberment, place the parts on ice. Transport him to the nearest veterinary facility.

Poison

Antifreeze, insecticides, cleaning fluids, chemical pipe cleaners, and some plants are poisonous to dogs, and can cause death. In certain cases of poisoning, induced vomiting is advised. Approximately four ounces of hydrogen peroxide poured down the throat will cause the dog to vomit immediately.

Do not induce vomiting if your dog has ingested any type of acid, caustic, alkaloid, or petroleum product, as these will burn the throat when expelled. Transport immediately to your veterinarian.

Poison Control Hotline for Animals (888) 426-4435.

The ASPCA staffs this hotline twenty-four hours a day to assist you with your needs.

Puncture Wounds

Any puncture of the abdomen or thorax should be treated by a veterinarian immediately. Objects remaining in the wound that can be seen *should not be removed*. Protect the wound by bandaging around the object.

Sucking wounds, or escaping air, must be sealed. Apply copious amounts of petroleum jelly or ointment to a cloth, and cover the opening. Transport to the veterinarian.

Shock

Exposure, blood loss, and injury are all reasons for a dog to go into shock. Shock victims should be kept warm, comfortable, and unmedicated. Dogs in shock will feel cold to the touch, display labored breathing, and may be unconscious. Transport to the veterinarian.

Snakebites

Dogs are capable of handling snakebites better than humans do. Due to the toxic venom injected by snakes, the tissue around the bite will die and be sloughed off, or may be surgically removed. Signs of snakebite are: bleeding and swelling at the puncture site and pain. Some dogs will appear tired and listless, and just want to rest. A dose of Benadryl at ½ mg per pound of body weight will aid in calming the dog and relieving some pain. Because snakebites are puncture wounds, infection, as well as toxicity, must be considered.

Stress

Stress can turn a normally calm, happy dog into an aggressive monster. Stress can be experienced from injury, exhaustion, environment, and pressure. Use caution when approaching a dog that is experiencing stress. Temperament changes are unpredictable.

Bibliography

Bauman, Diane L., *Beyond Basic Dog Training,* New York: Howell Book House, 1991.

Campbell, William E., *Behavior Problems in Dogs,* Goleta, CA: American Veterinary Publications, Inc., 1992.

Koehler, William R., *Koehler Method of Dog Training, The*, New York: Howell Book House, 1996.

Merck Veterinary Manual, The, Eighth Edition, Philadelphia: National Publishing, Inc., 1998.

Random House Webster's Unabridged Dictionary, New York: Random House, Inc., 1998.

Saunders, Blanche, *Complete Book of Dog Obedience*, New York: Howell Book House, 1981.

Whitney, Leon F., DVM, *Dog Psychology,* New York: Howell Book House, 1971.

LaVergne, TN USA
29 March 2011
221958LV00002B/48/P